MW00416184

Over Grandpa's Shoulder

Short Stories of a Family of 12: The Growing Up Years

Daniel W. Bushnell

of Fox Island & Lake Stevens

Illustrated by

Shahannah Bushnell

Copyright © 2019 Daniel W. Bushnell

All rights reserved.

ISBN: 9781091922754

DEDICATION

This book is dedicated to my Lord and Savior Jesus Christ, my wonderful wife, Joan, my daughters, Melinda, Kristin, Stephanie, and Brianna, plus all my grandchildren

FORWARD

I wish my grand and great grandparents wrote stories of their life. One of them went to Alaska with his new bride during the gold rush….but I know very little about his adventures and his life lessons. I encourage you, please write your life lessons for your children and grandchildren. The title, "Over My Grandpa's Shoulder" represents the weaving of my stories and life lessons throughout the first part of my life. The cover picture shows one of my grandchildren looking over my shoulder at our history. These stories were written for all my children and grandchildren, however, you have been invited into my life to look over my shoulder as well.

CONTENTS

PREFACE

As you read these short stories a common thread will present itself. That is how strong my mom is. God molded her and created a very special superstar. I love how she didn't seem frazzled when raising us ten children (eight boys and two girls)...five teenagers at a time for many years. On many occasions she had more teens at our house than her own. Mom was a surrogate mother to many. Everyone would follow her rules because she loved us all.

My mom calmed my dad after his recurring nightmares of being shot down over China during WWII. Mom is the one who taught other people's children all day, then came home to make dinner and help us with our homework. Mom was the strong one when my sister's 14 year old daughter (and her namesake) was killed in a car accident. My mother did her best to hold it together when she watched a drunk driver run over my little brother as he was on the side of the road. It was Mom who sacrificed her career advancement to be with my hospitalized sister who the doctors gave up on, then sent home to die. My mom had to try to sleep at night after finding out one of her sons was riding his motorcycle across the Narrows Bridge and got hit by a drunk driver. The only thing stopping him from going over the edge was the guardrail. It was her house that burned to the ground as she was in the hospital at my father's side when he took his last breath. Mom's the one who lost her husband after 55 years and came home to ashes, no pillow to cry into.

Recently I said to my mom, "You know how it is, a daughter needs her mother to help when she is pregnant or giving birth, so Joan goes and helps our daughters."

My mom looked at me and said in a sad tone, "Sorry Dan, I really don't know what it's like to get help from my mother when giving birth or raising children. When I was five years old my mother left home. I never saw her again until I was 55 years old. When I had Mary, your father was still in the Air Force and overseas. I was over nine months pregnant, had pneumonia, chicken pox and three small children (4 year, 3 year, and a 2 year old) to take care of. I was in the middle of packing the house because Pop was being transferred to Delaware. The doctor told me that my baby would surely die....I was all alone and I couldn't even talk to my mom. Mary was born four weeks late on May 9, 1955, with those chicken pox. So the first few weeks were not pleasant as she cried most of the night. I could not call my mom for help or anyone because we were new to the area and I didn't know anyone."

Mom had a tough life, but turned out with a huge heart. She had all the excuses needed to be a bitter woman, but she refused to take that path. When we had our children she came and helped us. Someday Jesus will say to her, "Well done my good and faithful servant."

The image of God carrying my mother is woven within the background of every story. I hope you are able to look deep enough to see them both.

SHOT DOWN IN CHINA
1944

Pop never intentionally talked about the war... this story was revealed during his funeral when my brother got up and told us the complete story. This is the only real story I have from my dad's childhood.

Pop was on a mission in his B-24 somewhere near/in China while in the fifth army, Robinson's Red Raiders, 22 bomber group. They received a bunch of flack and consequently lost power (I assume a couple of engines were hit). As they headed for home, it became apparent that they wouldn't make it over a mountain range unless the plane became lighter and very quickly. It was "all hands on deck" to throw out all excess weight. They barely made it over the mountain range, but now they needed to find some place to crash land.

During their briefings, they were told about an emergency "landing field" that would allow them to put down, but not enough runway to take off. They were able to get the plane on the ground. Being the engineer, Pop was assigned to blow-up and destroy the high tech bombing locator device called "Norton Bomb Sight." It was his responsibility to make sure it wouldn't fall into enemy hands. After everyone was safely off of the airplane, he blew it up and gathered the crew. As Pop started to explain to everyone that it's safest to head towards the hills, they could hear the Japanese coming towards them. He wanted to tell them not to head towards the ocean, since according to the survival manual (which he memorized), no one has ever survived by going towards the water…the enemy controlled the beaches. However, panic does strange things to people as many ran off. Pop told the remaining two flyers that he saw lights from a village on the other side of the mountain, but just didn't know if they were friendly or not. So they headed out.

Pop was a boy scout (received the highest award you can get in scouts, The Silver Beaver Award) and learned early how to run all day and night without getting tired. So he taught the others "the boy scout run." It was something like run hard 100 steps and walk 100. After the first day, they didn't hear the enemy and they eased their pace a bit…even took a rest after finding a strategically safe location. While resting, my dad couldn't help but ask the two men why they didn't run off towards the ocean like the others. One of them responded, "Joe, you have two knives strapped to your legs, and two 45's under your jacket…you are so brave, we just knew to follow you!"

Pop laughed and let them know that he didn't pack all this "fire power" because he was brave, but because he was scared. I guess that was the funny part of the story, but I digress. For two days and nights, they climbed through the jungle heading towards the light Pop had seen while dumping out the equipment.

They finally arrived at the village, but didn't know if it was in enemy hands or not. Pop gave his buddies one of his guns and a knife and told them, "Stay hidden and if I don't come out in 30 minutes, OR if you hear some warning signals, TAKE OFF!" Pop snuck into the small village and found a Jesuit Priest with a ham radio. After bringing his crew in, they called out and were rescued. What's interesting is that they flew out on separate P37's which usually have only one seat for the pilot, but the three planes they sent had two seats each. Pop assured the villagers that he would NEVER divulge the location or name of the village

Someday you will learn about the Doolittle raid and how the enemy burned AND killed entire villages of people that were suspected of helping the pilots that crash landed. The only part of this story Pop told us was that he was shot down and villagers in China helped him. Also, he told me about a student in my second grade class (1964) at Artondale Elementary School whose dad was the pilot that flew my dad to safety. Pop always told us that he would take the name of the village to his grave because that was his promise to the villagers…and he did. We will never know what the name of the village was and to honor him we will never look for it. He did receive the Distinguished Flying Cross, but I think it was for a different heroic act.

One lesson you can glean from this story is that my father lived because he read and put to memory the survival manual. Also, because he read this manual two others came out of the jungle alive. A survival manual has been passed on from one generation to the next that will guide all of us on how to live our lives. This survival manual is important and relevant; it is called the Bible. It is more important and can give you more advice than I could EVER try to pass on in this little book of memories. The Christian Bible is the word of God! If you ever want God to speak to you, read his words.

AN ONLY CHILD OF NINE
1959

Before Tony was born my mother always said, "Daniel, you're the only one of my children that is an only child...so you're the only child of nine. Tony wasn't born until I was 18 or she would have changed it to ten. She explained that the three older brothers, Joseph (six years older), Timothy (four-five years older), and John (three years older) would play together. Then came Mary (one year older), Daniel (me), and Laura (one year younger). The two girls would play together. Then Edward (three years younger), Lawrence (four-five years younger), and Thomas (six years younger) came along. The "three little boys" were too young to play with.

When we went on outings and the two trips across America we paired up. Joe was buddies with Ed, Tim was buddies with Larry, John was buddies with Tom and Mary was buddies with Laura. The older one was responsible to keep the younger one safe! It was quite a responsibility and everyone took their jobs seriously. If you notice, Daniel did not have a "buddy," but Daniel didn't really care as he would prefer to be alone.

Many times when Mom would look out in the backyard and… there I was, swinging or kicking the ball, or just playing hide and seek by myself (was kind of weird, but I always won!). One of my favorite games was to hide in the paper barrel.

One day Pop brought home a paper barrel and tossed it into the yard for us to play with. It was about three feet tall and 18 inches in diameter. After playing hide and seek by myself, I decided to flip the barrel over the top of my back and inch around the yard like a turtle with a top hat…but no one could see me (I would win again). I remember finding and collecting little maple helicopters (you may know them as maple seeds). It was like one of those bug vacuum cleaners, but instead it was me crawling around cleaning the play yard with a barrel on my back.

The next day Mom had one of those panic attacks that moms get when they can't find one of their children. After looking EVERYWHERE, she called the neighbor for help. The neighbor just laughed and assured mom that, "Daniel was okay." The neighbor explained that she was sitting outside being entertained by Daniel playing in the backyard by himself. "I've been watching him for hours while he was under the barrel very slowly moving from one side of the yard, bumping into the fence, turning the barrel around and moving back the other way. "I think he fell asleep under the barrel because it hasn't moved for some time now." Sure enough Mom picked up the barrel, and there I was curled up sound asleep.

I do remember Mary and Laura playing with me from time to time. It wasn't the same, however. I thought the girls were a bit skittish, since they would slide down the tall slide while I would climb the ladder and jump off. Then I got an idea! Back in the 50's all the girls wore long dresses that came to their ankles, even when they went out to play. So, to get them to jump off the slide, I came up with an idea. "Hey Laura," I said one day, "you are so lucky to be a girl. If you jump off the top of the slide your dress will poof out like a parachute and you'll float down to earth." Well, she went up to the top of the slide and apprehensively jumped. Her dress flew up into her face, and her little bottom led the way as she landed in the grass.

I thought, "Oh boy, am I in trouble!" But to my surprise, Laura shouted, "It worked, it worked!!" I was in shock. Well, maybe it did work. After all she said it worked so…

The next day I decided to let Mary in on the new discovery. She climbed to the top of the very tall slide and jumped off. Just like Laura, her dress flew up into her face and she came down like a rock…BAM onto the ground. I quickly said, "It worked, it worked!!"

However, she was not to be fooled, "NO, IT DIDN'T!" she exclaimed as she whacked me.

One day I had another idea. I said to Mary and Laura, "Hey, if you take one of your barrettes and put it into this mud puddle, when the sun comes out the barrette will still be there and all the water will be gone." Well, all the water was gone and the barrette was nowhere to be found. I didn't think at the time that the mud would dry around the barrette hiding it from view. Well, it was another failed experiment.

After reflecting upon my disposition, I came to understand why I was an only child of nine.

BIRTH OF THE BLUE BOMB
1950

Although you might think the old 1950 Dodge Panel truck wouldn't mean that much, but the family memories attached to it were rich and plentiful.

In 1950, Pop was told he would be stationed in Bermuda and that he would be promoted to Lieutenant. So he went down to Tacoma Dodge and purchased the 1948 Red Dodge Panel truck to use for camping, hunting and hauling stuff. Mom didn't care for the color, so Pop had it painted blue. Over the years its name had changed from the Bread Truck, to the Panel Truck, then to the Blue Bomber and finally the Old Blue Bomb. Pop had run into an issue that the truck only had two seats, so when Joe was born he installed two hooks through the ceiling that held a baby cradle. Joe swung in that cradle whenever they went camping. Mom became concerned since the cradle swung quite a bit more than they were hoping. When Pop got his papers to move they turned the truck over to Grandpa Ben (Mom's dad) who drove it all over Fox Island and to work. Pop had a surprise waiting for him when he arrived in Massachusetts; the military was downsizing and his promotion was withdrawn. He was disappointed, but such was life.

They refitted the old B-29's with scientific instruments where they would fly into hurricanes, gather and interpret the information, and report back. Pop always said, "You need to bloom where you're planted." Even though he was moved all over the world, he always tried to keep a positive attitude and took it as an adventure. I think he was glad he got to fly into hurricanes instead of in the Korean War. At the time everyone in the plane had to be a pilot in order to insure a safe landing in the event of an emergency.

The Blue Bomb was passed down like an old pair of jeans. Pop purchased it, gave it to Grandpa. Grandpa used it, then parked it, the blackberries took it, Joe resurrected it. He pulled it out of the blackberries, got it running and used it. Then Tim drove it when he was in driver's education (but had to purchase his own car after that), another brother revived it, but then got his own truck. Next Ed pulled it out of the blackberries and revived it again.

When Grandpa drove it around Fox Island, he had a unfortunate accident with a horse. Since Fox Island was open range, people just let their horses and cattle run wild. After all, there was no need for fencing since we had the beach and the bay to keep the animals safely in the area. A horse ran right into the side of Grandpa Ben near the Bulkhead Road. Since it was "open range" the accident was deemed Grandpa's fault and the horse owner sued him.

DOG ATTACK
1959

I had to rack my brain to figure this one out. Why is it that when I came around the corner of the tool aisle at Home Depot a pang of fear shocked my body? I froze for many seconds until a large dog passed by. Then it dawned on me. When I was three years old our dog attacked me, got me down and started biting me, and it hurt! When I was only four years old our neighbor's German Shepherd bit me on the leg two different times. It has been the story of my life. Dogs seem to like biting me! Some people say that, "Dogs know mean people and will attack only those type of people" or some ridiculous notion like that. I love animals! I raised cows, goats, pigs, rabbits, chickens, cats…etc. I taught animal science for many years. I don't hate dogs…well, I don't like dogs that bite me or any mean dogs. But dogs in general…well, I really love golden retrievers, labs, and Irish setters.

Recently, I was walking on a trail to a lighthouse on the Oregon Coast, when a wiener dog walking with its owners just jumped over to my side of the trail and bit me. It ripped my nice pants and almost broke the skin.

I flashed back to Delaware…down I went head hitting the sidewalk which sounded like, "a dropped rock." That's when everything went quiet and everyone was gone. What happened? Where did everyone go? My body told me to breathe, so I did. Taking a large breath, everyone seemed to come back. There was John, Tim, and Joe. Joe was having a difficult time holding me on Tim's back as he was trying to carry me home. John cried out, "Why aren't his legs working!" Other neighborhood children just stood there staring in disbelief as I faded in and out of consciousness. Everyone was gone again and it was quiet until…my body told me to breathe again…so I did, letting out with another loud wail. This time Tim was on my left side and Joe was on my right carrying me like expert Boy Scouts until…I fell backwards and hit the sidewalk again, but this time just my back hit (they weren't Boy Scouts yet). Everyone was gone AGAIN! Breathe… I felt like throwing up, but I breathed anyway, each time letting out a blood curdling scream. Now John had my back, Tim and Joe carried me and I have no clue where the dog went…all I knew is that I was almost home. Yes!! There was Mom coming out the door…now I am safe and everything went quiet again as Mom carried me home.

We had gone a block from our Delaware home and had just crossed the street. That is when our dog, who was hooked on a 20' chain, decided to run. Tim was very strong for a seven year old and was able to hold the chain so Spot could only go into a large circle. Well, when the chain came John's way he simply hopped over it (John is a great athlete), Joe did the same, but when it came to me…well, that's when my feet were knocked out from under my three year old body. Well you know the rest of the story.

TEACH YOUR CHILDREN WELL
1959

In 2013 a famous person, Phil Robinson of Duck Dynasty, made a comment that he never saw any racism growing up in the south. He continued by explaining that he and his black friends worked side by side in the fields. Everyone was poor. This caused quite an uproar from people who hated him (those who hated him because he does not believe homosexual behavior is correct). They now had a reason to call him a racist.

As an older person I can understand what Phil was trying to say about the black South. I lived in the South in the 50's and early 60's too. I never saw any mistreatment of black people. BUT THERE WAS PLENTY!!! Later in life, when I was older, my mother told me of a time a neighbor lady came over and said that others were "talking." Since my mother let a black boy play with her children, no one was going to let their children play with us.

My mother responded, "Good, I wouldn't want your type of influence polluting my children." So we continued to play with the black children. I saw no mistreatment and he didn't either.

My mother also went to an all black college in Delaware and there was a lot of racism against her. One time the professor locked her out of the class because he didn't like white people. She had A LOT of good friends there and refused to become blinded by the hate others directed at her. She didn't want to become blind to all the good people and consequently become a morally bankrupt person.

Two lessons can be learned from this experience: One: People who dislike you will always twist what you say to reinforce their preconceived idea. If someone says something negative and not true about you, they will usually believe it without ANY evidence. I find myself doing the EXACT thing I accuse others of doing to me. We must be VERY careful to constantly examine ourselves to see if our motives are pure. Two: When a person is raised and lives their entire life fighting prejudice, but then are called a racist, it makes one ponder and fight less hard. In other words, don't alienate people by calling them hurtful names or assuming the worst.

Be very careful you don't get into the rut of hatred. Hatred tints your view of the truth and refuses to allow you to see, listen, understand, or love many people around you. It lessens your ability to live life to its fullest. I married someone who nearly always sees the best in people. She listens to what they say and weighs their words, meanings, and feelings. She seeks the truth and believes the best in people. I hope all my boy grandchildren find a bride like Grandma Joan. She is a real woman of God!

A POSITIVE COMMENT
1960

I can remember very clearly some positive things my dad said to me. I know people usually remember the things we wish we could take back. I know if my dad knew those negative things he said hurt, he would like me, love to undo them. However, that's not what I am writing about here.

One time in Delaware it was snowing really hard. It started piling up and no one was home except Mom and four or five of us children. I was thinking, "I can clear the snow off the sidewalk." So, this four year old grabbed a snow shovel and started in. To be quite honest, I couldn't believe how easy it was as I worked for several hours, meticulously scraping every inch of the sidewalk all the way down to the road and up along the public sidewalk until I reached the neighbor's property.

Mom was very pleased, but I really don't remember what she said until Pop came home. "Who shoveled the sidewalk for me?" he declared.

Mom looked at him, then me and said, "Daniel worked on the sidewalk for hours…didn't he do a great job?"

Pop declared that, "It was a VERY good job!" and again questioned, "Are you sure you were able to do that ALL BY YOURSELF? It is a GREAT JOB. I just can't believe how good it is!"

I was beaming with satisfaction…I was able to do a good job clearing the sidewalks for Mom and now Pop! Later he told me that what I had done was as good as a grown man could have done.

When in eighth grade, I started rebuilding the barn and eventually had a small general shop, a drive-through to work on my VW bug, a milking parlor for the cows, and a hay loft that I eventually moved into.

I think I can overlook the many things Pop said that I am sure he wishes he could take back, BUT, I refuse to overlook the positive things he said to me. BTW, I became an agriculture teacher and one of the many classes I taught was Lumber Construction. Raise up a child in the way he should go and when he gets old he will not depart from it. My parents had very watchful eyes on all of the 10 children. They allowed us to explore our talents and encouraged us. They did their best to give us the tools we needed to flourish.

As you can imagine, with so many family members our septic system had a tough time keeping up. So one day I dug a ditch and laid piping from the upstairs laundry room all the way through the parking lot and into the garden. In the garden, I dug several holes deep enough to hold a 55 gallon metal barrel. This allowed us to send all the water from the laundry room to the vegetable garden, which helped preserve the drain field. After I was done, Pop did his inspection. For some reason he really liked the box I made to hide the pipe that came out of the side of the house. I overheard him tell Mom something like, "Daniel did a great job transferring the laundry water to the vegetable garden and you should see the box he made along the side of the house. I think we have a carpenter in the family." From then on I looked for building projects around our home.

Joe was the firefighter, paramedic, and later started Tacoma Recycling. Tim was strong and could fix anything on a car, including body work (he had to do a LOT of body work due to his fast driving). Tim became a police officer, then an owner of Roto-Rooter franchise, John was the BEST athlete I ever knew, BUT was not allowed to play due to the length of his hair. He later became a logger and now installs heat pumps. Mary was a fabulous cook and when she was nine would cook dinner for our family of 11. She graduated with a degree in Food and Nutrition. I became the farmer and loved marine biology, but got a degree in Agricultural Education (later became an associate HS principal). Laura was very good at sewing and later became a Special Ed teacher, then a massage therapist. Ed was another mechanic but took it to a new level. He became VERY good at it. He is now a mechanic at Boeing and helps teach Boeing employees. Larry was a good actor and I always saw him as the star of many school plays. His degree was in Japanese Language and Literature and he works buying and selling fish for Trident Seafood. Thomas was a first string star athlete on a team that won the State Football Championship. Tom also became a state wrestler and loved to debate everyone on every issue at anytime…he became a lawyer. Tony was still too young to find his niche at the time, but later became a Physician's Assistant.

A VISIT FROM GRANDPA & GRANDMA
1960

I was so excited back in 1959 or 1960 when Grandpa Ben and Eleanor Kibler drove all the way from Fox Island to Delaware just to visit us (who knew that in four short years we too would move to Fox Island). Although I was excited to see them, I was more fascinated by their Siamese cat. They let it out of the van to relax on our city size front lawn. I watched as a neighbor's large German Shepherd started freaking out, barking and foaming at the mouth. Then it broke loose and ran right at the large, country cat. Not sure if the dog or I was more surprised to see the cat turn towards the dog and run straight for it.

The cat's eyes turned blood red, its hair was standing on end, and her claws looked like sharpened knives. The dog came to a skidding stop only to run smack dab into the cat's claws. He then turned and took off running faster than I have ever seen a dog run. "Yipe, Yipe, Yipe!" and away went the dog with this large Fox Island country cat close on its tail. The cat had no fear as it chased the dog all over the neighborhood. Years later, the story is still told of how our grandparents brought a cougar into the city and terrorized all the dogs (they were embellishing...it was just a regular West Coast, Fox Island house cat).

Grandma Eleanor told us that cats on the island had to fend for themselves. She told us children about a time the cat took on a raccoon, "more fierce than a little East Coast city dog." Little?? I always thought that German Shepherd was huge. On cue, just as Grandma had finished the story, we all turned our heads to look out the large picture window. The dog was running by with the cat in hot pursuit. After what seemed like hours, the cat came back to our house, ate its dinner, and left again.

We started playing in the backyard when there was a commotion in our neighbor's yard. This time the cat had jumped the fence and was chasing the dog around in its own backyard. The dog finally got out and started running down the road with the cat chasing him.

I think the cat had more fun that week than us children getting to see our grandparents for the first time.

Comments from other family members:

Joe: I remember the cat and the neighbor & their dog, Rex. Rex liked only Mike, the oldest son next door. Grandma and Grandpa Kibler came over in a Ford van that had the engine between them and the steering wheel over the front wheels. It was an early camper.

Mom: The Siamese cat met his end in Florida. He took on an EIGHT FOOT alligator and lost. Those Fox Island cats had NO fear!

BUGGY BOOMER
1960

When it comes to raising a child in the way he should go, my mom and dad nailed it!

Insects, arachnids, and bugs in general…they fascinated me. If any of the neighbors' pathway stones were flipped or out of place everyone knew they had a visit from "Buggy Boomer," a term of endearment created by people perfectly casting my three year old personality.

The name Buggy was obvious…because of my fascination with all small creatures. This fascination was modified when we moved from Delaware to Fox Island, Washington, in 1964. My curiosity expanded to include ALL marine invertebrates. The name, Boomer, came from how I "learned" to go down stairs…When I was one or two years old, I was very impatient with the time it took to go down a flight of stairs. So to speed things up, I would walk to the top of the staircase, buckle my knees, and fall. A loud thumping echoed throughout the house causing everyone to come running… "Daniel fell down the stairs AGAIN!"

"Who moved the gate?" would be the next thing yelled. With four older siblings it was difficult to keep the stairway gate in place. And there I would be sitting, at the bottom, looking up, smiling, and saying, "Boomy down." My mother finally folded a thick quilt and positioned it on the cement pad in the basement. So that is how I got the last part of my name.

Buggy Boomer would go from one neighbor to the other asking if they needed someone to pick the Japanese beetles out of their rose petals. I would get paid a penny for each Japanese beetle. It was the job of my dreams, catching/collecting bugs and getting paid for it! For my neighbors, well the women couldn't resist paying this six year old for getting those darn beetles until…well, until they saw their flowers. I was so determined to get EVERY last beetles that I took EVERY rose petal off EVERY plant and picked them apart one petal at a time. By the time this locust was done they wished for the Japanese beetles instead of the neighbor's Buggy Boomers Beetle Service. I made a penny and a disaster.

One day I was looking through the bushes for bugs when I came upon an anomaly. There was a large round bulge about the size of a small golf ball. Not thinking much of it, I picked it and secured it in my daily collection of goodies. When I got home I started sorting, taking all the isopods and putting them in one jar, ants in another, and so on. I secured every lid knowing that Mom is never pleased when she finds a worm out of a jar in the house. When it came to the small golf ball sized egg case I was out of lids. No worries, nothing was moving, so it probably didn't need a lid.

We were eating dinner one peaceful evening when a very small praying mantis dropped from the ceiling onto my dad's plate. "Hey Buggy Boomer, looky here, we have a visitor." I jumped from my chair and ran over to get a closer look. Sure enough there was a magnificent 3/8 inch praying mantis. Its claws were too small to hurt me. I had experimented with larger ones and man did I get a quick lesson and a band-aid.

Joe yelled, "Look" as he pointed to the ceiling. We all quickly noticed that an invasion was taking place with thousands of small praying mantises. They started dropping like paratroopers from the sky. A scream destroyed this magnificent bug catching moment as one landed in my little sister's hair. Until that moment I thought to myself, "This must be what heaven is like…as all the bugs were coming to me!" Others saw it as an example of a horror movie…all the creepy insects coming after them. Pandemonium reigned, as all my brothers and sisters were frantically trying to dislodge all the bugs from their food!

I glanced at Pop, and it appeared he had a smile on his face as he said, "Buggy, let's say you and I build a cage for all these mantises." It took me a long time to figure out why Pop was so calm. Evidently, earlier that day he was in the cockpit of a bomber, full of fuel and bombs. The engines were running and he was on the tar mac in position to take off to bomb Cuba. Everyone was coiled tight…he was aware that Cuba had nuclear weapons and as soon as his bombs were released Cuba would destroy the Eastern seaboard…that would mean an end to his family.

Making anything with my dad, collecting bugs with my family, getting to look through the cage at praying mantis for hours…it was a dream. One day as I was in my usual trance, staring into the bug cage, Pop came up to me. "Daniel, I called the college and the science department needs praying mantises. What do you think if we, you and I, gave them to the college?

We could do it together." I think it was just the thought of getting to ride with Pop, all by myself, all the way to Delaware College that excited me most. THEN I saw their bug collection. A new reason to be excited filled me as, according to Pop, I started jumping on one foot then the next back and forth…my eyes bulged and mouth dropped. Every time I flipped a rock, looked in the bushes, or ran through a grassy field with an open water bucket, there would be another world of wonder and new bugs to see. However, this insect collection was all of it times ten.

As I began thinking back to the praying mantis excitement, other events start filling my mind. We were visiting my grandparents, Bill and Esther. They lived near Puyallup, Washington, and had a very large yard. Since it took me hours to explore every inch, I took Ritz crackers (in a box) as a snack with me. On this wet, rainy journey I came upon a yellow jacket's nest. It looked inactive at the time, (later I learned that bees stay out of the rain), so I picked it and stuffed the entire nest into the box.

I finally came into the house to watch TV with "Bill" (my grandpa who did not want us to call him grandpa) and my other siblings. During a commercial, Bill went into the kitchen to get a snack. "Oh," he thought, "some crackers would be just perfect." He didn't notice that the misshapen box had a very large bulge in the center. He also didn't hear the angry buzzing noise emanating from within.

I learned some new words that day as Bill reached into the box… (or as he would like to describe it as a buzz saw (a much edited version of his words)… We went from a peaceful, drizzly, lazy Sunday evening football watching day to stark terror. I think everyone, except Pop, was screaming. Pandemonium and VERY angry bees filled the home as people were diving out the windows, others got stuck in the doorway, and still others locked themselves in the bathroom while others were pounding on the door to let them in. I learned what panic meant and even at the age of six I vowed to be calm while others ran around. Pop was calm and sat there very still as others freaked…he had seen panic before. Pop opened all the windows and doors and systematically smacked yellow jackets with a rolled up newspaper until the house was safe again.

I never felt welcome at Bill and Esther's home. One day I remember hearing Grandma Esther say in exasperation, "Why does something ALWAYS get broken when those kids come around!!!" Hearing this left a big negative impression on me. My brothers have very different memories as John would visit many times just to drive their riding lawnmower. It caused me much thought as I wonder what I might have said in exasperation that might have an effect on a child's life. I think the only way to fix it is to apologize and spend time with the one you hurt. Later in life, when Grandma was dying of cancer (I didn't know it) she knitted me a thick sweater which I still have. Perhaps this was her way of apologizing for time away from us grandchildren.

HIT BY A CAR
1961

I think it was the culture of the time when I got Joe, Tim, and John in trouble with the nuns…boy did they get, "the what for." Later in life I heard from Pop how they dealt with friends dying. Pop and I were on a trip together, just us. This was very rare, but he knew how important farming was to me so we headed out to Wenatchee to look at farm land. Ended up, (I was 17) I didn't have enough money at the time… $100 per acre was out of my range, but I knew how much I needed to start saving. On the way he told me about his officer training and how his friend was killed while flying the B-24. I just couldn't ask any questions, as he was obviously still hurting.

Many miles later he just picked up where he left off. "I landed the plane and got out…" I never asked him a question about the war again. He did receive the Distinguished Flying Cross for something, but not sure if that was it or another time.

It was only about 15 years after WWII, when so many adults were still being tough that I got Joe, Tim, and John in trouble with the nuns. Joe was 12 and the fastest bike rider, so he was in the lead, Tim was 10.5 and second, John was nine and was next on his bike, Mary was seven and I was six bringing up the rear of the bike "parade." We were on our way to a special mass that was being held at night. Every child attending Holy Cross School, "had to be there!!" I was doing my best to keep up and it finally looked I was gaining on Mary. I got a full head of steam, took the corner wide, all the while leaning my bike like a racer, but…just as I blew past the stop sign…WHAM!

I didn't notice the car until the bike flipped up over the hood. I can remember my face pressed up against the right front tire, but I thank God that the tire wasn't turning as the car went skidding along the highway with my face pressed up against it. Everything went from a peaceful bike ride to a very loud ruckus in milliseconds. Panic struck the three big boys as they rode as fast as they could back. Flying into the house, they screamed to Mom, "Daniel was killed by a car!!!"

I wasn't killed, I wasn't even hurt, just a little shaken, didn't even cry until… well, remember it was the 1962 so the people picked me up and put me in their car to drive me home. This would be the first of many times I would see a look of complete despair, fright, and anguish on my mother's face. As we came closer to home, I saw my mother running towards us. I remember very clearly she was running very fast and tears were flowing, her mouth was open and a moan was bursting out of her mouth. We stopped, seeing her face… well, needless to say I started crying too, as it hurt to see my mother in such anguish. I learned that it hurt me more to see the pain my mother went through than the pain of getting hit by a car. Oh, I almost forgot, my brothers didn't show up for the special mass. When they explained why, they were sent to the office and "raked through the coals for missing the mass." It's too bad this happened as there are so many good nuns. That is how I got my brothers in so much trouble and they missed mass.

WHO'S WATCHING THE OLDER CHILDREN
1961

The big boys (Joe, Tim, and John) knew just how to keep me from venturing into the swamps. "Daniel," they would say, "you don't want to go into the swamp...there's quicksand." Quicksand!!! My eyes went VERY big. Now I didn't want the big boys to go into the swamp. They would come back with exciting exotic animals (exotic to a five yr old). We would empty out the metal laundry tub and fill it with water. They would put the baby ducks, turtles, crayfish, salamanders, small fish and all sorts of neat things in the tub. I would stare and play with them ALL day until Pop came home and would take them all back.

As a child, it never seemed to matter my age, I always admired, respected and was awed at the big kids. Two incidences really brought it all home for me. A third incident taught me I could be an example for children my own age.

Example 1:

Dover Delaware 1961: When I was five, Tim told me that in order to be in the advanced sledding club, I would have to ride the sled with him on my back. We would have to go down a very steep hill that flattened at the bottom before the three foot drop onto the frozen lake. My hands stuck to the metal as I lay down. Tim grabbed the wooden steering handle while lying on top of me and down we went. The "hill" seemed more like a cliff as we picked up speed. I squirmed to escape, but Tim's weight held me in place. Before we got to the small cliff, we were going like a gazillion miles per hour, then went airborne over the frozen lake. At this point the sled, myself, and Tim all separated a bit before hitting the ice. First the sled hit, then I hit the sled and almost knocked the wind out of me, then Tim completed the job with a powerful belly flop onto my back. Now we were shooting out to the center of Silver Lake, where the ice became dangerously thin. Thank the Lord before we got too far some big teenage boys were playing ice hockey. As we passed through their game, they all took turns trying to slow us down (and save our lives). We plowed through them like a bowling ball, as one after another were knocked out of the way until…we hit Big Bobby Jones and thud! The sled stopped, but Tim and I went spinning another 20 feet and into their net. Tim always seemed big, but these teenagers were giants next to his 10 year old frame. I would do anything the big boys told me to do, well, at least I'd do it one time. I never went sledding down that hill again, but John and Tim did. I think Tim enjoyed disturbing the ice hockey games…I saw it totally different.

Example 2:

I was a very young six year old when starting the first grade, my first time. On this particular day I brought my special Donald Duck ball to play with at lunch time, but during recess my ball flew over the fence and down into the ravine behind the high school building. It was rumored that there was quicksand at the bottom and "NO ONE should go down there!" Not sure if it was a made up story by the nuns or if there was truly quicksand behind the Holy Cross School. Needless to say, I never saw anyone dare to go down into the abyss. I just collapsed to my knees and cried, knowing that I would never see my special ball again. An older boy came over to console me in my tears. He thought I might have fallen and was hurt, but this was much worse. Between sobs, he was able to determine the source of my anguish. The next thing I saw was this big Christian boy climb over the fence and head down towards the quicksand. My eyes grew wide and my mouth dropped as he disappeared down into the "valley of death." Moments later he reappeared with my ball in hand, threw it to me from the other side, then leaped back over. I wanted to be like that big boy when I got older. I was so excited to get my ball, yet never went back to thank him, but I wish I had. I vowed from then on to do my best at helping younger children.

Example 3:

I learned you can look up to people your own age, like the way I looked up to Steve Carpenter. I met Steve during my first day of second grade when he saved my life! I think I am getting ahead of the story, so I must go back and let you know what might have led up to this moment.

It was 1964 and after 21 years in the military, my dad decided to retire and move the family from Dover, Delaware, to Fox Island, Washington. Unbeknownst to us, there was quite a turmoil going on about the Fox Island School and the new bridge. Now that the bridge was built and the new Artondale Elementary School was opened there wasn't a need for a school on the island. Besides they claimed, "There really aren't enough children on the island to justify another school."

Then we moved onto the island! People were jubilant! Someone was even planning a parade, but that could or couldn't have happened since there were so few people on the island at that time. Yep, at one time we were heroes with nine children moving onto the island as now they couldn't keep the school closed "because there weren't enough children!" Being a "hero" was very short lived…the Peninsula School District announced that since we moved on to the island there were now too many children for the small school, so the school was closed permanently. We went from "heroes" to "goats" overnight. The gossipers would say, "Because of the Bushnell's large family, they closed our school." So all the children were transported everyday to the mainland from that day on.

HELPING GRANDPA
1962

Although my Grandpa Ben and Grandma Eleanor Kibler are no longer with us, they must be laughing right now. When I was six years old, we drove from Delaware to Fox Island for a visit (and to see the Seattle's World's Fair). When visiting his old log home between Fox Point and Toy Point, he told all of us boys (there were seven at that time) not to touch the bricks around the fireplace. He had just set them in place and the mortar had not yet hardened. BUT, he never told us why we should not touch them. Being a very curious child, I had to pull one of the bricks out. It happened to be a lower one. Needless to say, there were a lot of bricks that came my way and so did the paddle.

Now here is why they are laughing. My grandson, Daniel is very curious too. I had set aside a few hours each day to work on my bride's new covered porch. I finished digging two footings, set one pier block in place and pulled part of the old concrete sidewalk out. I was done for that day and went to cut lumber on my saw mill. Came back the next day...well, Daniel had moved the pier block I had positioned, leveled and adjusted, filled in the hole that I had prepared for the second block, and broke my best shovel.

He said, "The first block I moved because I thought I could help. I filled in the hole so Grandma won't fall in it...you know she's very old. The shovel broke when I used it to pry up the concrete sidewalk. The concrete wouldn't move so I jumped on the handle...and it broke." Yep, Grandpa Ben is definitely laughing right now!

There's really no reason to get upset. I am so thankful that Daniel lives next door, that he wants to help, that he thinks independently, even though sometimes he's wrong, and that he's MY grandson! It also reminds me of when I worked for Farmer Browne.

Farmer Browne told me of a time he had a "partner" that did nearly NOTHING! His partner was a lazy man that drank, swore, and got mad too much. He explained that they worked "together" replacing glass in homes and buildings around Tacoma in the late 1930's. Well, Mr. Browne had started putting in a window when it just broke on him. He knew his partner would be very UPSET because he always cursed and swore whenever something went wrong. Mr. Francis Browne was also very, very smart and he thought about it before telling his partner.

This is what he told me, "I knew he would start swearing at me and become VERY upset, so I thought about it and got the jump on him." I said, "Do you know why you never make a mistake?"

He said "No."

"It's because you never do anything!" "My partner didn't say anything when I told him about the broken window."

Mr. Browne was very careful when I broke something on the farm or made any other mistakes. He would say "Well, it's okay, don't get down on yourself. It only shows me that you're doing something, not just sitting around." I was always VERY hard on myself when I broke something or hurt someone.

I believe there is always a reason for something breaking or going wrong. The Lord is in control and there's no good reason to get mad, swear, or become angry when something goes wrong. Besides, when something breaks, your children and grandchildren will learn from your reaction. What is the Lord trying to teach you when he allows…

I am very thankful for Farmer Browne's modeling.

1962 WORLD'S FAIR
1962

Each step up the 18' ladder with a pack of 3-tab roofing over my shoulder reminded me that it won't be long before I just can't do this type of work. With a bam, I flipped the pack down onto the roof. Eleven done and only five more to go! I started down again when I was shocked with a surprise tap on my head. I thank God my reaction was to hold tightly to the ladder instead of jumping from it. "What could have tapped me?" I thought to myself.

Looking up I saw my six year old grandson, Daniel, smiling down at me. "Grandpa, look at this big playground." He swung his arms out and twirled around to encompass the entire roof of our two story home.

My memory flashed to the 1962 World's Fair and I could swear my dad was laughing in the back of my head. I too was six years old and we had just travelled with all nine siblings across the United States from Dover, Delaware, to Seattle, Washington.

I remember the doors to the elevator opened and I ran onto the observation deck. I looked down to see where we had been and to get a better view of the line at the bottom. In order to get the best view, I had to climb over the top rail of the Space Needle and crawl out on the fins where I sat. I was in total control and thought nothing of it until my dad told me to come back, "Now!" So I did. From that point on I was not allowed to leave Dad's side and it was many years later I found out why. My best teacher was a little warming of my behind.

So now here I am, on top of an 18 foot ladder looking up at my namesake with my dad's laughter echoing throughout my brain.

FIRST TIME IN PUBLIC SCHOOL
1964

It was September 1964, when just one year ago I had been in a classroom with 59 other students at Holy Cross School in Dover, Delaware. Now I was in public school, sitting at my desk and looking around. Here the children were all sitting down very haphazardly. I sat down as I was taught, my back straight as an arrow, my hands folded on the desk, my feet FLAT on the floor, but my eyes and head were not facing forward. I sat in amazement looking around as Mrs. Fisher called each child to introduce himself, and to tell us what they did during the summer. NONE of the children stood when talking. When my turn came I quickly snapped to attention. Standing up and addressing the teacher I said, "Mrs. Fisha, my name is Daniel William Bushnow and our family moved to Fox Island frum Dova, Delawaa this summa. I have six brodhas and two sistas." My Delaware accent was very deep and I saw every child's eyes on me as I spoke. As Mrs. Fisher thanked me and had JUST finished explaining that I didn't have to stand each time I talked, another adult walked into the room. I quickly snapped to attention and stood. I looked around and was wondering, "What's wrong with these people! I hate to be them when the principal finds out!" (I thought they must be new).

Later I found out my third grade sister, Mary, had a very similar experience. She explained that because we had so many children in our classes in Dover, Delaware, they had to make sure no one misbehaved. I thought, wow, my sister Mary, is very smart. It was interesting to see the other children's response to my standing up when an adult walked into the room. Some started to stand, but quickly noticed no one else was standing. Other children just became wide eyed at this spectacle. It made me wonder if that same adult walked into John, Mary, or Laura's class, I bet they stood too.

<u>Recess:</u>

Mrs. Fisher pointed to another student, John Ford, and said, "John, you're going to be Daniel's friend. He is new and needs someone to point out the boundaries of the playground." I thought it was a bit strange since the playground at Holy Cross was a very large asphalt parking lot. Perhaps there was quicksand on the other side of the fence like at Holy Cross. John took me around and showed me this very new and strange habitat.

In 1964 a small grassy playfield surrounded A LOT of wooded area. John walked me to a four stranded barbwire fence and we followed it through the brush to the corner. He pointed out that we were not allowed to go on the other side of the fence, since there is a very mean, large, and dangerous bull that lived just over the hill. If you go into his field, he will chase you and he is very fast. I found out the next year that it was true, but that's another story. Then John led me to…well, near the corner post in the back of the wooded area. You could just make out a driveway (which later became 64th Ave). We couldn't get real close to that fence, since there was so much underbrush. We made our way to the south side of the field and along the road. He explained that we were not allowed to play on the road (the speed limit was only 35 back then… before it was changed to 50). During the school year, I found that we played most of the time in the woods, running on trails, making forts, and picking blue huckleberries. Recess was absolutely a blast.

In 1967 the principal, Mr. Baldwin, informed us that the grass part of the playground was going to be expanded into a much larger baseball field. He wanted us children to have a say in which way we wanted it to expand, towards the road (which is now a 50 mph highway) or towards the thicker part of the wooded area. He explained that it would mean there would only be a small strip of woods to play in. Under the guidance of Mr. Duga, our fifth grade teacher, we discussed the pros and cons of the decision. I am sure other classes had the same discussion, but the final decision was to keep away from the highway and expand the field back and towards the right. We missed the deep woods to play in, but there was now a new large field.

Many nostalgic memories were made on the playground, like the day I met Steve Carpenter, the boy would become my best man at my wedding. It was my second day at Artondale as all the children ran out to play. I was new and there was a bully who wanted to let me know he was boss of the playground. He came over to me and pushed me down, then started kicking me real HARD down a very steep hill. I must have been crying very loudly, since many children stopped and just froze, not liking what they saw, but were too afraid to stop it. I looked around for John Ford, but had forgotten that he was absent that day. I felt so alone at this new school, new home, new environment, thousands of miles from where I had been and I really didn't know anyone. As more and more kids gathered around, I felt more and more alone. All my brothers and sisters had different play times so there was no one to help me. The schoolyard bully was having his fun.

Then the fog parted and light shown through as Steve Carpenter came running up to the scene! The bully was a head taller than me and Steve was a head shorter than me, but he was tenacious. Even in second grade, Steve would stand up for people and do the right thing. This time he happened to stand up for me, when NO ONE else would! I was shocked to see this very small boy (should have been named David) run up to the bully and yell, "STOP HURTING HIM!!!"

The bully just looked at Steve and laughed, "What are you going to do pipsqueak? You're next!" I had a great view of what happened next. With fist clenched, Steve jumped up into the air and smacked the bully directly in the nose (Steve had to jump since the bully was so tall). The bully's eyes opened very wide and he turned and ran.

As he was running away, Steve proclaimed, "If I see you picking on ANYONE else, I'll finish you off!" The crowd of first and second graders cheered as he helped me to my feet. From that day forward, I tried to emulate Steve's example and he was one of my very best friends. We didn't have adult playground monitors back then. Children were expected to play nice with each other and if there were problems we just had to figure it out.

Here is an interesting twist to the story about the bully. Do you remember reading about the time my dad got shot down in China? Here's where that story has a thread attached to that playground bully. When my dad got picked up in the P-38 it was the bully's dad who rescued my dad. He was the pilot of that P-38! I wish his son wasn't a bully, as I think we could have been best friends. In 1964 the great Alaskan earthquake happened and the bully's dad moved his family to Alaska. He was a civil engineer and was assigned to help redesign a city. I think the bully was relieved to move to Alaska after being bested by my good friend, Steve Carpenter.

ATTACKED BY A CAT
1964

One day I heard another one of my brothers yell. This yelling business was all new to this eight year old, but that quickly changed as more and more of us stepped into our teenage years. Every Sunday evening our family would look forward to watching the Walt Disney TV show. On this particular day one of my older brothers wouldn't let me pet the cat. Fact is, he put the back end of the cat towards me and it was nearly in my face. I think the show was about a cross eyed lion named Clarence. I was becoming frustrated because I was trying to watch the show, but my brother kept moving the cat so the tail was in my face. Out of the corner of my eye, I could see my mother giving my brother the stink eye, but she didn't say a word as to not ruin the peaceful family moment.

I really didn't think about the consequences when, with all my strength, I pinched my right suspenders all the way open. I then lifted the end up and clipped it onto the cat's tail. Right during family time the cat freaks out! All the claws within her four paws started spreading my brother's shirt. With those claws still out, it jumped onto my brother's head, did a dance, then flew off the back of the couch. The suspenders stretched further than I thought they could before slipping off the cat's tail, springing back at full force, and smacking the back of my brother's head. This all happened so fast no one knew or saw what I had done. I quickly hooked my suspenders back onto my pants and played innocent. I think the only person who knew what happened was my mom and she didn't say a thing.

My brother started yelling at the cat, as all my other siblings looked on in shock. Pop said, "What do you think got into that cat?" He looked at my brother and said, "What did you do?" My brother started crying as a small trickles of blood beaded up and dripped down his face. I felt sorry for him a little, but kept remembering how he was putting the tail of the cat in my face. It was all the persuasion my mom could muster to convince my dad that the cat's didn't have rabies.

HIGHLY EXPLOSIVE
1964

In June of 1964, when we first moved to Fox Island we found an old train caboose in the woods just south of our new home. I had no idea how they got it on the island or when. Trees had grown up against and all around the train car. It became a very nice playhouse for us children as there was a kitchen and playroom. It seemed that we younger children played in it all the time, but one day we invited Tim to join us. Tim discovered two very strong wooden boxes under the counter. We'd seen those boxes before but hadn't pulled them out to look inside yet. On the outside of the boxes were written some words which Tim read out loud, "Dy-no-mite." He very cautiously looked in one of the boxes and found it full of one inch by 12 inch sweaty dynamite sticks. Tim quickly and loudly told us to, "GET OUT OF THE PLAYHOUSE, NOW!" We couldn't figure out why he was so loud and adamant about us leaving, but leave we did. I watched as he carefully and cautiously walked backwards out of the playhouse and ran to find Pop. My dad took Tim's word and did not go back and investigate. He told all of us children to keep away from the caboose; then he called the bomb squad at Fort Lewis, to handle the explosives.

It was dynamite alright. Evidently, my Grandpa and Uncle Ben were hired to clear the hillside in Tacoma called Brown's Point. They cut all the trees and built a skid road to slide the logs down to Commencement Bay, where they built a log boom. They then went back and used the dynamite to blow up the stumps. It was likely the dynamite had been sitting in the caboose for around 25 years.

My mother explained why Tim yelled when he found the dynamite sticks. She said, "The bomb squad said that those sticks of dynamite were very unstable, and if one of the children had pulled out the box or jiggled it, the entire caboose would have been turned into toothpicks. The only thing left would have been a very large hole." She continued, "If you six children, (Tom, Larry, Ed, Laura, Dan, and Mary), were still in the caboose when the dynamite exploded, you would not be alive today. Tim was concerned that you were in danger so, that's why he yelled. You should give him a big hug for saving your life. Tim is a hero." I guess that's a good reason to speak loudly.

FRIENDS AT ARTONDALE ELEMENTARY
1965

A lot of things have changed since I was in elementary school. Now you're not allowed to bring a knife to school and the teachers can't lead a prayer before lunch. We were also different. I remember walking down the road from our home, heading up the hill on Mowitch Dr, becoming thirsty and taking a drink from the crystal clear water flowing along the roadside ditch. There were very few houses on the island and even fewer cars. While riding the bus, sometimes all the children would start an all bus game (never knew what the game was called, but it was fun).

One time Gary got on the school bus with a big cardboard box. We kept asking him, "What do you have in the box?"

He wouldn't say a thing except, "It's for show and tell."

We were so excited, it was hard to wait, but wait we did. When it came time for Gary to do show and tell, all the children and the teacher were at the edge of their seats. Gary slowly carried the big box to the front of the room, sat it on the floor, slowly opened it up and took out a full grown chicken. That's right, a chicken! I couldn't believe what I was seeing. It would be VERY difficult to catch ANY of our chickens as they were so wild. I had never seen a pet chicken that was so tame!

Gary set the chicken on the table and started explaining how he raised it from an egg and how it follows him around the yard, how it sits on his lap when swinging, and so on. The teacher used this teachable moment to explain imprinting. My desk was right next to Gary's and I was in awe the rest of the day. ALL DAY his chicken just stood there on his desk, watching him do his school work. It didn't jump off and run away or even make a sound; it just stood there watching.

During recess he carried it around, then demonstrated to the crowd of children how the chicken could swing with him. He set it on his lap and pushed off. There he was swinging with the chicken on his lap. Then we tried the merry-go-round and the chicken just stayed with Gary. The chicken didn't cluck, nor try to run away. It just sat with him.

Here's another example of how things were different...One morning while walking to Artondale Elementary from Wollotchet Bay, my friend, Wade, came upon a dead skunk. It was right around the time Davy Crocket, or it might have been Daniel Boone, came on TV. ALL the boys wanted a coon skin cap with a tail. Well, Wade was no different, so he took out his buck knife and skinned the skunk, tied the furry feet together, kept the tail attached AND... you guessed it, put it on his head. He walked into our 3rd grade class and EVERY boy was envious until he was sent home for three days: NOT because he was in trouble, NOT because he came to school with a knife, but because it took three days to get the smell off him. Those were such fun days...during the time I had no clue how much fun we were having. Now, we have some GREAT stories and those days live on in those stories...which are also fun!

DEATH BY BEES
1965

I remember the very first time that I met Marty. I was with my brothers, John, Tim, and Joe fishing off the ferry docks down at the old Fox Island store. Marty and his older brother, Kevin, came up and met us there. I think my brother John had invited them since they were new to the island and Marty's brother was his age. Anyway, when Marty introduced himself I noticed that he had a cleft palate and spoke with a high pitched voice. I very innocently asked him why he talked that way. Holy Cow!!! It was like I had just set off all of my grandpa's dynamite. Tim became so mad, he almost threw me off the dock. John scolded me and Joe told me how stupid I was. Seriously, it was just an innocent question from a young nine year old boy who, I guess, should have known better. When I got home my mom laid into me too. I felt so sorry for Marty; I really didn't want to make him feel bad, but I must have.

The next thing I knew, we were like best friends until he moved. One day he was teaching me how to be an Indian and walk very quietly through the woods. He was very good at that. Seriously, he was so light on his feet that you could not hear him as we made our way through the woods. We came to this old tree that was down and like a feather Marty floated up over it. I thought to myself, "That's a lot of work to climb over that big tree." So I decided to go under it and pop out on the other side. I only got part way when my head hit a large yellow jackets' nest. Well, no more playing quiet Indian! Marty and I started 'playing' which little Indian will be able to run through the woods fastest without hitting a tree, getting tangled in blackberry brambles, or getting another sting.

I forgot a very important part of this story. I had a serious allergy to bees and my syringe and medicine was at home on the other side of the island! Marty's mom didn't drive or didn't have a car so she, Marty, and I ran over to Mike Ford's house. It seems quite comical now, but at the time Mrs. Ford and Mrs. McKeag started freaking out. Perhaps I shouldn't have told them that I would have 15 minutes before my throat swelled and stopped my breathing and in 30 minutes my heart would quit pumping.

I don't think the car had seat belts, but it didn't matter to Mrs. Ford because she was going to drive as fast as she could. Thank goodness back in those days you could drive anywhere on the island and it would be rare to see another car. Most of the time people who had cars would drive down the center of the road (to better avoid deer), plus there weren't any dividing lines anyway. Then it happened! We had just passed through the dip by the Fox Island school and started up the long 9th Ave. hill when Marty said, "I think he's starting to swell up!" I don't think I was, but it really freaked Mrs. Ford and Mrs. McKeag. I think back and I can't help but laugh. They let out with a gasp and a scream (not a high pitched scream, but more of a growl). Mrs. Ford punched the accelerator all the way to the floor, but because the hill was so steep the car didn't speed up, it just made more noise. I don't think the car had a muffler which only made it louder, not faster.

We got to our house (on 14th Ave.) and Grandma Kibler, who was the island nurse, stood there with syringe in hand. She gave me the shot as Mrs. Ford collapsed with her head on the steering wheel. I felt bad for her and Mrs. McKeag, having put them through this ordeal. As you may know we have EIGHT boys in our family, so for my mother it was just another normal day…she was not fazed in the least.

So, a very important life lesson was to be careful what you say; your words may hurt someone. Another lesson that I used as a vice principal was when two students didn't get along give them an option. They could be suspended or sit next to each other all day doing their school work, then eat lunch together, then write ten things they like doing and one thing they wouldn't mind doing together. There was more to it than that, but I hope you get my drift. Although the second one was not my life lesson, it was that the adults thought I didn't like Marty when I asked that ignorant question, but all of us came out better because I had.

Another memory was going to Westport with Marty. I don't think I had ever been so far away without at least one of my brothers with me. While in Westport, Mrs. McKeag and her sister, Mrs. Ford, went shopping from store to store. It was also the first time I had EVER been in a gift shop! (Mom was smart not to take us eight boys in one). All sorts of small trinkets were displayed, but as you know, we came from a very poor family so looking at things was the only thing I could do. Then, out of the blue Mrs. McKeag said, "Daniel, what would you like?" I picked a pennant that had the words, "Westport" and a picture of a salmon on it. I still have that it.

A side note about Grandma Kibler: When anyone on the island needed medical help or had a question Grandma was called. She was like the first stop emergency care on Fox Island, that now-a-days seems to have sprung up everywhere, except Grandma did not charge. She was often called in the night and ALWAYS responded. It was a long trip to any medical care - two toll bridges and an hour or more away. If someone called an ambulance, it would be nearly two hours or more before you would arrive at the hospital. If you called Grandma you didn't even need to tell her your address…she would know and show up at any time you needed. That was before Dr. Lawrence moved onto the island and he gladly took on this responsibility.

When I look back at all the physical changes that occurred on the island, it hurts. However, these changes don't control my feelings…what should NEVER change is the love islanders should show to each other and their island. I know this sounds corny and I don't think of myself as a touchy feely person, but if people want to have their own good memories…keep an eye out FOR each other…enough said…back to another Fox Island story.

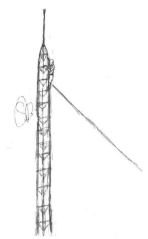

CLIMBING THE RADIO TOWER
1965

My grandfather, Ben Kibler, was the strongest man I have EVER known. I guess you really had to be strong to have the job of topping trees. Mom had explained that he would pick the tallest tree, usually on a hillcrest and climb up over 100 feet and cut the top off. Grandpa would then take out a sandwich and eat his lunch while sitting atop of the pole.

After lunch, he would then attach anchor cables at the top the "pole" and a cable that ran to another pole on top of another hillcrest. The donkey engines would pull a pulley along that cable (which they called a skyline). This would allow the loggers to pull the trees up and out without making a skid road…but they still had to make a logging road, where they could get their equipment in and out. It's interesting all the things that are named after logging practices of the past. Where I live now we have an elementary school named Hillcrest and another one named Skyline. I often wonder the best way of helping people understand their past. Then I wonder how many things I don't know that have a direct connection to the past. Whenever you think about others, it's important to honestly reflect upon yourself. Many times what you see in others is really a reflection upon yourself. Reflect honestly!

One of my brothers just adored Grandpa Ben. Many times he would get up early, leave the house, and just show up in the front seat of Grandpa's 1948 Dodge panel truck. Grandpa would get in the truck, look over at him, then start it up and drive off to work. Grandpa was not a talker and neither was he, so off to work they went. He would watch Grandpa climb the very tall trees, run a donkey engine, or fall a tree. During lunch Grandpa would sharpen his saw as my brother ate his lunch.

One time in 1965, my 11 yr. old brother decided he would be just like Grandpa and climb to the top of a pole. I need to explain something; Pop was a ham radio operator and built a 100 foot radio tower in our back yard. Pop had the power company put in a very tall pole that had a block (pulley) attached to the top. A cable ran from the radio tower, to the pole, then down to the bottom where it wrapped around two giant nails. Pop would unwrap the cable, attach it to the bumper of our truck, and lower the tower down to lean on the roof of the house. While the tower was on the house, Pop could do any adjustments or replace the antenna. Then he would have Mom drive the truck forward and the radio tower would slowly rise up into position.

Okay, back to the climbing the pole. So my older brother shimmied 10 feet up the pole, just like Grandpa, until he got to the foot pegs that were sticking out of both sides. What he didn't notice was the cable that held the radio tower was now knocked loose and laying on the ground. He made it to the top of the ridge pole and noticed that the radio tower was higher than he was, so he headed back down determined to get higher, just like Grandpa. So, straight up the 100 foot radio tower he went. Upon approaching the top, he saw Pop's car coming down the driveway. Hoping not to be caught, he stayed perfectly still, so "maybe Pop would not notice" him up there. BUT, he did!

"You come down from there RIGHT NOW!!! I will see you IN MY ROOM!!! NOW!!!" So my brother headed back down the tower, all the while anticipating the "motivation" he would receive when he got to "Pop's room."

Do you remember the cable that he had knocked loose when climbing the ridge pole? Well, unbeknownst to him that cable held up the tower he was JUST climbing. That's right, this 11 year old was at the top of a 100 foot tower that was teetering. He got to the ground, took a few steps, and the tower came crashing down onto the house. First thing my brother thought was, "Oh man, I am in sooooo much trouble now!!!"

Pop flew out of the house screaming in fear for his son's life. He kept yelling his name over and over, "Where are you?" …No, no, no!!!!! Then he yelled my brother's name again! My brother heard Pop and knew he would be better off not hiding.

So, out he came and said, "I am here." Pop ran over and hugged and hugged him. My brother couldn't figure out why Pop was hugging him instead of giving him spankings, which he knew he deserved.

Rest of the story, he became a logger, just like his grandfather before him, BUT, now they use tall metal towers instead of topping trees. So, for the most part, my brother keeps his feet on the ground.

GOING CAMPING...WITH ELIZABETH
1965

It was the best option. Elizabeth, our goat, was still in milk and there was no one on Fox Island in the 60's who had time or knowhow to milk her. So, we took her camping with us. While traveling, we had her in the camper with Joe, Tim, John, Mary and me, being too civilized to have the goat ride in the seats. Pop always drove and Laura rode between Pop and Mom in front. Ed, Larry, and Tom, rode in the back seat of the pickup (Tony wasn't born).

We developed a great system for the disposal of goat beans as we traveled down the highway. When Elizabeth's tail popped up and wiggled in the air, we knew she had to do her duty. Joe, being the oldest, would open the back door to the camper. Tim, being the strongest, would move her back to the opening. John, being the next oldest, would watch the "littler children" so we wouldn't fall out. I also need to let you know about my dad's driving habits. Pop was a very courteous driver. He took his time and always drove five miles under the speed limit. Fact is, he almost got his first ticket when he was 72 years old, but they waived it. On the one lane highways, he would ALWAYS pull over and let other cars pass after just a few gathered behind him.

On this particular day, we were heading to a campsite at Mount Saint Helens. We didn't know our parents were also going to spread Aunt Helen's ashes on her favorite mountain. Anyway, we were heading down the back road highway going a bombing 55 in a 60 mph zone. Pop had just pulled over to let cars pass and had not gone more than three miles when an older model muscle car came right up to our bumper. I happened to be looking through the camper door window and saw the guy's face. He

42

looked mean with his scowling face. He was definitely NOT happy.

I have to tell you that this is a true story; I am not embellishing ANY part of it. I don't think all the elements of this story will EVER line up again. My dad had seen the car pull up on his tail and was looking for another place to pull off when, unbeknownst to him back in the camper, Elizabeth's tail went up. Joe, being the oldest opened the door and I saw the guy's face turn from angry to inquisitive. Tim, being the second oldest but strongest, backed the goat so her rear end was sticking out the back. John being the third oldest, would watch the younger children (Mary and I). Being the youngest one in the camper, I just sat there and continued to look at the "mean guy's" face. At first the guy's face was mean, then inquisitive, then shocked, and when Elizabeth let loose with hundreds upon hundreds of goat beans his face turned to stark terror. The beans started bouncing onto his car, but when he slowed they would bounce off the pavement, THEN hit the hood of his car. As if on cue, Elizabeth then squatted and let loose with gallons of "water" (I think she was holding back for the last several miles). The urine took the same course as the beans, but caused his windshield to turn yellow. His wipers went on, but only to smear beans and yellow "water." He slowed WAY DOWN....

When Elizabeth was done, Tim moved her all the way back into the camper, Joe closed the door, John stopped watching Mary and me and we all went back to what we were doing.

Pop had noticed the beans bouncing 10, 20, or 30 feet into the air behind our truck and was trying to figure out what was happening, when it dawned on him! He let out with one of his full fledged belly laughs and Mom sat there looking at him and asked, "What's so funny Pop?"

He just said, "Oh, I can explain later."

When we finally got to the state park, we drove around the camping circle looking for a place to camp. Back in those days you didn't need reservations, they just had A LOT of extra spots for people. On this particular day, however, there was only ONE spot left and we took it. Then everyone started piling out of the truck and camper...I noticed the people in the neighboring sites staring at us as we got out. First it was Tom, then Larry, then Ed, then Mom, then Laura, then Pop, then Mary, then Joe, then Tim, then John (Their eyes got larger and larger as more and more people poured out of the truck; then I got out and following me...was Elizabeth, THE GOAT). I don't know what got into everyone at the park, but before long there were A LOT more campsites open. I think people react differently when they see a lot of children. Some see it as an adventure, and life being breathed into an otherwise boring day. Other people see it as a burden and a lot of noise. Maybe it was the goat. We will never know

CATCHING MY FIRST SALMON
1965

Mark Miller, Joe, Tim, and John were also fishing with a pole, but I had a 25 cent hand line in the water. Mr. Walker, who owned the store at the dock, sold hand lines that were wrapped around a plastic holder. The line was really a type of special string that appeared more like construction line. I caught a salmon on that hand line. The salmon was jumping around, but we didn't see it because no one ever thought you could catch a salmon on a hand line. We were all at the end of the dock watching as the other four used fishing poles. Well, until Mr. Walker, who was watching us from his window, came down and asked us, "Whose line is this?"

Joe or Mark said, "Not ours." They didn't know it was mine and they didn't want to get into trouble.

I spoke up and said, "Mr. Walker, that hand line is mine; I am sorry, I'll pull it in right now." I really didn't know what I had done wrong, but his voice was very stern. He let us fish off his dock, buy stuff from his store, and above everything else he was one of the nicest person we knew. Back in those days you gave respect to EVERY adult and you ALWAYS told them the truth.

He said to me in a very firm voice, "Pull it up!"

I felt like I was really in trouble this time! I quickly did as he commanded and there...as the end of the line appeared...I yelled, "A SALMON!!!" Mr. Walker got a big grin on this face and started laughing as Joe, Mark, Tim and John all ran over to look, and we all started shouting with excitement.

Evidently, Mr. Walker's family was watching from their home and wondering why we just let the fish jump around for such a long time. It was so tired when I pulled it up to the surface that it just floated there and when I pulled it onto the dock the tail never even flapped.

KIDNAPPING ON FOX ISLAND
1966

Your Great Grandma Diana will "never forget this story." It was about your Great-Great Grandma Kibler's peacocks, a boat, a "fight" and guns. Living on Fox Island had MANY advantages. The air was clean, it was VERY quiet, and we were away from gossipy and noisy city neighbors (although there was plenty of Fox Island gossip).

As you know I had seven brothers and we did not always get along. Fact is, we did our fair share of fighting. But after the fight it was like a beautiful new day had dawned…no one seemed to remember and life was "all good." Not everyone understood our symbiotic life style, but…well. We were strong, strappy boys growing up on an island where we could yell without bothering anyone, spit on the grass (if it wasn't worn off from us playing hard) without a neighbor complaining, or go exploring the woods and get lost just for the fun of it. One day we were minding our own business, fighting in the front yard. Grandma Kibler's peacocks were perched in a madrona tree that bordered the property. While we were fighting, the peacocks started their infamous calling, "Heee UH, HEE UH, HEEE UH." We were so used to the sound and so into our boy fighting/wrestling that we didn't visualize the scene that just unfolded on our quiet little island. I need to stop here to describe the front yard. It was about 100 feet wide and 30 feet from the house to the edge. No one ever passed "the edge" for it was a cliff that went down between 30 to 60 feet. We never measured it, BUT it was definitely high enough that you wouldn't want to fall!

On this particular day, there was only one fishing boat taking advantage of the calm, sunny weather and abundant fish that lived at the edge of our yard. As the boat trawled by, fishing line bobbing in the quiet still water, our fighting scene started playing out. At first the lady in the boat heard the peacocks' screaming with their hair curdling announcement (evidently she had NEVER heard a peacock before and never raised boys). With her imagination at full bloom, she witnessed two people fighting "for dear life," at the top of a cliff, on the end of a very secluded island. Blood was flowing; screams had pierced her peaceful visit…she knew exactly what was happening. Someone was KIDNAPPED on an island that almost no one lives on!!!! She quickly got on the radio and reported the incident, "He was fighting for his life and bleeding before the big one flipped him to the ground and carried him away from view. I could hear him screaming for help. I have NEVER heard such blood piercing screams before. He was trying to escape and ran to the edge of the cliff, saw me and started yelling for help….I thought the big one was going to throw him over, but he saw me and just pulled him back out of view. I could still hear the screams…I think he might have killed him!! PLEASE HELP!!!"

It took the "Swat" team quite a while to drive the 30 miles from the city to the island, circle our house, and start calling out instructions through the blow horn. We boys had forgotten all about the earlier wrestling and were happily playing downstairs. Then we heard something that sounded like interference on the old TV set, but the TV wasn't on. Perhaps Joe turned on one of Pop's ham radios and was listening? There it was again! I went to the sliding glass doors, pulled back the drapes and thought I'd have to go change my clothes. The police were pointing BIG guns at the house…they were everywhere! Being the big, brave boy I was I started yelling up to Mom, "MOMMY!" By then Mom was already talking with the sheriff. Just then the peacock started screaming again and everything came into perspective. The sheriff was also raising boys in the country and just seemed to know what happened. Also, it was nice he went to the same parish in Gig Harbor (Saint Nicholas).

A CHRISTMAS NOT TO REMEMBER
1966

Mom was about to complete her Master's Degree at University of Puget Sound when Laura became ill with some rare disease related to Muscular Dystrophy. The doctors tried all kinds of experiments, but could do nothing for her. EVERY day Mom would drive to Madigan General Hospital to be with Laura, then home. Many times I went with her and wondered how she could see through those quiet tears welling up in her eyes, then streaming down her cheeks as she drove up I-5.

As a nine year old, I had no idea of how Mom's life had just turned upside down. She only had a week or two to finish that last class, then receive that coveted Master's Degree, but she dropped out to be with her ill child. I've seen my mom frightened, like when I got hit by a car, but I have never seen her so sad. It wasn't that piece of paper declaring her completion of a Master's Degree that brought on those tears. It was the slow, but steady decline she saw in her precious daughter, Laura. Laura became weaker and weaker to the point she didn't have enough muscle to lift her arms. The only way she could get around was in a wheelchair that someone had to push.

Soon it would be Christmas 1966 and I am sure Mom was not ready. The only bright spot for her was when all the children went out in the field, cut down a Christmas tree and the support that was given from Fox Islanders. We decorated and did all we could to make it a good season. We became jubilant when the doctor said Laura could come home for Christmas, but it didn't stop those tears Mom tried to hide from us. She was ALWAYS positive and did her best to keep the family in good cheer, but I saw her when we drove home and could tell her heart was broken. Yes, the doctors said we could take Laura home for Christmas, but what

Mom and Pop didn't tell us was it would be her last one. The medical staff explained that Laura would probably NOT make it to Christmas, but she may as well die at home with her family around.

Somehow my Cub Scout den mother knew of the pain Mom was going through. She had our whole den working together to find ways of making this a very special Christmas for our family. I remember a small tree she had us decorate that could sit on Laura's night stand. Other people of Fox Island did many other things to help, but I can't, remember them now.

Each morning my dad was apprehensive about opening Laura's bedroom door to check and see if his seven year old girl was still breathing. Finally, they broke the news to the entire family and we showered Laura with attention and prayers. Mom and Pop prayed for Laura! It was nerve racking for all of us, I could hear my mother's muffled sobs every night after she tucked Laura in and helped her say her prayers.

Laura lived to Christmas morning. Pop went into her room to awaken her. He pulled back the covers, gently, wiggled her shoulders and said, "Merry Christmas, Merry Christmas Laura, wake dear…it's Christmas." It was really hard on Pop as he agonized all this time, thinking to himself, "was this the day?" She just laid there too weak to move, but her eyes sprang open and she shouted in her sweet, exciting, child's voice, "Christmas!" Pop's relief was apparent as he carried her in his strong arms then gently set her on the couch in front of the Christmas tree. I saw something that day no one in our family had ever seen before, Pop with tears in his eyes. We had a wonderful Christmas. I don't know what was given or what was received, but I did remember we were ALL together for this one last Christmas.

A couple days later it appeared to me that she was getting stronger. Day after day Pop would enter her room to see if she would wake up and day after day her eyes would spring open as she said, "Good morning Papa." Within a month Laura was able to lift her arms. When Mom took her back to the hospital the doctor was flabbergasted to see that she was still alive AND her improvements. He told Mom to, "keep her home surrounded by family, and keep praying, it was the best medicine for her and that she was recovering at home, not the hospital."

Well, that was in 1966 and my little sister, Laura, has totally recovered… completely. I don't care what people say, I believe in the power of prayer. Sometimes God says no, sometimes He says not now, and still other times He says YES. I like it when he says yes. What I do know is that He wants us to pray.

The gift of our Savior's birth is the BEST Christmas present I have ever received and the gift of Laura's recovery is the second. Fifty-two years later...still the same, my two favorite gifts.

Tough experiences will help you later in life. It builds character and will get you through tough times and prayer will help you get through life ALL the time. To this day I find it hard to express myself verbally, in order for you to know my heart and what I am feeling, so I write it down. Grandchildren, keep an eye out on your own feelings and see if you can express them better by writing.

A note from Laura to Dan 52 years later:

Dear Dan,

This is the Christmas that I do remember. I remember every detail. I remember the welcome home signs, and a book of get well cards that a first grade class from Harbor Heights made for me. Mr. Wiles the custodian at Artondale Elementary School gave me a transistor radio! But I remember most that you held my hand and helped wheel me to the living room to see the tree. I think it was the first time we had the tree upstairs at the Fox Island house. I don't apologize for believing in the power of pray. I know it is true and I have experienced it working within me. It was like the healing power was multiplied by each one of my siblings. So God's own power times eight! Plus Mom and Pop who were praying with the power of 10...at least.

I remember on Christmas morning Pop sat me on the green couch next to the arm rest and Mom was on one side of me on the couch and you, Dan, sat on the arm. I was like one of my dolls. You can sit them down, but they slowly fall to the side. Well there I was so happy to be surrounded by my brothers and sister. As I started to drift to the side, your gentle hands propped me back up. The raucous ritual of opening gifts was as lively as normal, but for me it was the most memorable.

DECORATING THE CHRISTMAS TREE
1967

I could hardly believe that my siblings and I were actually decorating the tree without one cross word. Nice music was playing as we strung the lights and other decorations. The tree was nearly complete when one of my younger siblings brought out the ugliest "ornament" I have ever seen! There were two Styrofoam balls. The larger one had an old, broken and dirty, seagull feather sticking out and a toothpick that allowed the smaller ball to attach (I guess it was supposed to be the head). Out of the head, two toothpicks, representing a beak, stuck straight out. Underneath this monstrosity was a very weak spring attached to a clothespin which gave this thing a constant movement type motion. It was ugly and distracting.

Perhaps I should have let him put that thing on the tree, however, the tree was beautiful, and this ornament would be a major example of ugliness. I said, "You can't be serious? You are not thinking of putting that disgusting piece of junk on the tree are you?" Maybe it was the way I said it, I don't know. All I knew was he let out with a high pitched squeal that could put an elephant down. Mom came flying around the corner to comfort the injured sibling.

"What's wrong?" asked Mom.

He let out with the most pathetic whiny voice, "Dan won't let me put the ornament I made in Scouts and gave to you on the treeeeeeeeee, sniff, sniff!"

"Dan," Mom said, "Let him put the beautiful bird he gave to me on the tree."

"Mom," I explained, "I don't see any beautiful bird!"

Another squeal, "Eeeeeee!"

"Dan," Mom insisted, "LET IT ON THE TREE!"

"See Mom, you didn't say beautiful bird!" I quickly pointed out.

"Pop!" Mom called out quietly.

"Oh," I quickly said, "Mom, you don't have to call Pop, I'll help him put his … his… thing on the tree. Here, let me help you."

You would never want to disturb Pop with such a trivial thing. He always had a way of spanking first, then asking questions. No matter how many calluses I obtained, he always found a way of making it sting.

I was about to help him put the piece of junk on the back branch when he pranced over to the tree with a "got yah" smile on his face, looked at me, and started clipping it onto the one branch, the only branch that stuck out into the middle of the room. The one branch that every tree has that you say, "I am going to trim that branch off," but you never do. Well, I couldn't believe it! Now when anyone walks into the room, the first thing they see is an ugly bird that is in constant motion. A dirty, ugly, partly decomposed broken seagull feather, stuck into something that someone was trying to make look like a bird. This was going to be the worst Christmas ever.

Every night before Christmas, I would awaken with visions of an ugly bird swinging towards me and knocking me down. Every night I would go to sleep thinking….how can I get that bird off the tree, or how will I get even with him? Christmas Eve was no different until 3:00 AM when I woke with a start! An idea came to my little mind.

Sneaking into the kitchen, I opened the refrigerator door and took out the tarter sauce. While placing the jar under my arm, I grabbed a large spoon. Hoping beyond hope that Pop was asleep, I listened. My dad was very big so I could hear his deep rhythmic snores as many of the curtains in the house moved in concert to his breathing. "Please, Pop, don't wake up! Please don't wake up!" I said to myself as I feared getting caught before it was time.

While the jar was still under one arm, I maneuvered his largest package directly beneath the bird ornament. Ever so quietly, I unscrewed the jar and started scooping and dumping the sauce onto his Christmas package below.

The next morning I was up by 5:00 and watched as he came skipping into the living room, took one look at me sitting prim and proper on the couch, then at the tree. "Screeeeeeeeeeeeeeeeeeeech…." The scream was so loud and long that the tree started to lose its needles.

Mom came running around the corner, all the way saying, "What's wrong, what's, wrong?"

"Look what Dan did to my packagggggge!"

I put on the most innocent look I could and explained. "I didn't do it! It was the bird; I told you not to put it on the tree. Now look, it made a mess all over your present."

Just then I heard a thump, thump, thump, and the house shook as Pop arose and headed my way. I could feel my heart pounding to the steps of the big man as he came for me. Thump, thump, thump…. Pop picked me up by the back of my neck and I floated into the bedroom. This was the first time in my life I didn't feel any pain when getting spanked and I think my dad had a half smile on his face!

SCREAMS IN THE NIGHT
1967

I think it was the summer of my sixth grade year when Mark Miller and I decided to go camping. Many times we just decided to go a mile or two through the woods with sleeping bags and just roll them out when it got too dark. One time we decided to "camp out" in the back pasture near 14th Avenue. During the summer, the back pasture was used to grow the hay that we fed the cows during the winter. So we didn't have to worry about being stepped on while we slept. BUT, what we didn't figure was Grandma Kibler's peacocks.

Mark and I had laid out our sleeping bags, gone and played some more...we had climbed to the top of a very tall tree (about 130 feet) that was near our sleeping bags. After getting to the top, I would say, "Ready, Set, GO!" ...and we would race to the ground. I found that if you go out farther from the trunk you can go faster and if you put your arms out it will slow and control your fall. As I think back I would say, "Yes, that was one of the dumber things I did"...BUT, I won. In a boy's life winning really meant more than you could ever know. To win you always remembered, but to lose you always forgot.

As it got darker, we decided it was time to sleep. The dew had already collected on the grass and outside the sleeping bags. It was easy for us to fall asleep, but unbeknownst to Mark, he snored. Something else was happening while we were sound asleep. Grandma's peacocks, which were VERY curious animals, had seen the two big bags in the pasture. They flew out to where we were sleeping to get a closer look. I don't know what possessed them to do that. I didn't think they were nocturnal, but there they were walking around innocent kids, sleeping in the middle of the pasture in the dark of the night.

I think it was Mark's snoring that nearly ended our lives, as it startled the peacocks. And when peacocks are startled, they let the whole world know as they yell, "HEEE UH, HEE UH, HEEE UH, HEEEEE UH." Right in our faces! I don't think I had EVER been more frightened in my entire life, before or after that incident. I think I am still feeling the scare brought on by those peacocks. I think Mark too awakens from time to time with the nightmare of that very moment. Have you ever tried to escape from a sleeping bag while you're panicking? If anyone was watching on that dark, dark night they would have seen something funnier than the three stooges. We finally escaped from our bags, almost at the same moment and headed for the tree. I don't know why we went that way, but we did. I got there first, but Mark started climbing up my back which sent me to the ground and all in the same instant I got up and started up his back trying to climb the tree. This happened two or three time before I got a grip on the branch and scampered up with Mark on my heels.

We didn't stop until reaching the top of that 120 foot tree and only wished it was taller. With our eyes wide we held on, breathing hard, very hard. Finally I got the nerve to ask Mark, "What, what, what was that?"

He replied, "I don't know, but I am not going back down there!" We spent the rest of the night at the top of that tree, too scared to climb back down. That was the first time in my life I didn't mind not winning a race. If Mark wanted to race back down, I'd say, go ahead, you win!

FISHING & HERRING
1967

Being able to walk out my front door and fish anytime was wonderful. My fishing pole was kept at the ready, all the time. A friend of Mr. Browne taught me how to catch trout with a red and white striped "daredevil lure." We also fished for perch off the bottom of the concrete dock. You could no longer walk on the top deck of the dock, since it had rotted away years ago. The bottom supports were well under water except at the lowest of tides. There were nine pillars with several horizontal concrete supports that went from one pillar to the next. I remember carefully walking around on top of those supports and looking down at the clear water below. The dock was constructed on the drop off and it was fascinating to see all the way to the rocky floor, but it was always too deep to see the substratum where the drop off ended.

I don't think anyone ever went fishing for perch, so they became very prolific and LARGE, but they were the most finicky eaters of all the fish. I can remember putting a small shore crab on the hook, lowering it down, bumping the nose of a perch, but it wouldn't take the bait! However, at JUST the right time, only five minutes before and five minutes after the tide changed they would start biting. Looking down into the water the perch looked to be 24 inches long, but after pulling them out they'd end up 16" (still very large for a perch). The most I would catch is two since the tide changed so quickly and soon the concrete support would once again disappear under the surface with the current so strong you couldn't stand there anymore.

I also remember the very large barnacles that grew on the dock supports. They must have been at least three inches in diameter and three inches tall. Other adventurous parts of the dock were these six inch construction holes left in each pillar. It was not uncommon to look underwater and see octopus nestled inside. The massive amounts of calcareous tube worms kept us and the perch entertained as they would pull their feathery filters back at the slightest hint of danger. Okay, I must admit, I could watch the show for hours if the tide had only let me.

Another favorite fishing spot was the herring docks, also known as Mr. and Mrs. Walker's old ferry landing or the Fox Island store. It was a great hang out. The Fords, McCaves, Mark Miller and other friends lived nearby. It was the same dock I where I caught my first salmon, but that was nothing compared to Mr. Walker's 50 pound king that I watched him catch. He had taken off all the weight, attached a live herring on the hooks, and let out the line. The herring took it farther than anyone could cast and it wasn't long before a 40 or 50 pound King Salmon found the lone herring and swallowed it. Back in those days hooks were priceless to us and I remember reaching my arm all the way in the fish's mouth trying to detach the hook.

Mr. Larry Walker used to service the boats that would come by for fuel. That was his job, to run up and down the old ferry dock every time someone wanted fuel or herring. Many people would come by just to pick up herring from the Fox Island store because you knew it was fresh. As a child it was fun seeing all these new people; it was like you could stay in the best place ever (Fox Island) and the world would come to you. Mr. Walker was VERY patient and always allowed us boys to fish off his dock, but we always had to clean up any fish we'd catch.

Everyone knew how Mr. Walker kept the bait fresh, except maybe the State Department of Labor and Industries. But things were pretty laid back on the island and I'm not sure that folks in Olympia really knew much about Fox Island until one of our islanders became governor.

Larry would keep the live herring in a big container that was lined with fishing net attached to the docks. He also made a metal fish bucket that was secured with a rope under the ramp. If you wanted a pound of live herring, Larry would come down and dip his net on a long 30-foot pole into the container and bring out a whole bunch of herring. Sometimes people wanted dead herring so they could easily hook onto their line. That was fun to watch. Larry would take a pail of salt water and dump it into a specially designed metal bucket called "the bucket" that he had constructed. Then the herring would be scooped into the net. After the customer confirmed that that was the amount of herring they wanted, he would pour them into "the bucket." He was always very careful to make sure we boys would stay, "way back." Fact is no one was allowed near "the bucket" during this part of the process.

Mr. Walker would bend over and grab the end of a very long extension cord that went from the store, under the road, down alongside the ferry ramp and up in the vicinity of "the bucket." With a quick motion, Larry would grab end of the cord that had jumper cable type clamps attached. He'd attach the clamps to "the bucket" which had two studs, one for each electrode. This would cause 110 volts to travel through the water that contained the herring. "The bucket" would literary spark to life. And the herring inside, well, they would do just the opposite. It was strange that they would all be facing the same direction in "the bucket " as Larry applied the electricity, all the herring would jump in unison. Then he would unplug it and repeat the procedure two or three times. Each time, the herring would jerk, but less and less. Finally, after all the zapping and jumping, he would lay the two clamps down, pick the bucket up out of its holder and pour the herring into the customers container.

BLUE BOMB REBORN
1967

Grandpa Ben used it for his logging work and it was full of chainsaws, ropes, pulleys, blocks, engine parts for the saws, files, and assorted tools. He used it for many years and then in 1964 when we moved back from Delaware to Fox Island, Joe noticed that the truck was just sitting there with blackberries growing up through the engine compartment and just stuffed with "junk." So he adopted it or maybe it was the other way around; I'm not sure. So that was the start of the Bomb's third "owner."

The condition of the panel truck was atrocious. Weeds surrounded it, blackberries grew up to the windows, and there were signs of vectors in the back. The engine was frozen, the battery cracked, and the floor was covered with grease. It was a mess. So Joe started cleaning it out. Joe recalls it very well. Some of the rat droppings were so big that he joked about being afraid he might be confronted by a man-eating rat at any moment!

Joe pulled the truck up to the house with the bulldozer and started working on it. First, he pulled the heads and poured WD-40 down the cylinders. No luck. So he removed the head and beat on it with a 2X4 and a sledgehammer. No luck. So Joe then dropped the pan and loosened the pistons. Still, no luck. So he just did a short block. Pop and Joe took the engine out, loaded it into the back of the pick-up, and hauled it into the only NAPA auto parts store which was at the bottom of South Tacoma Way. They had all the equipment that could do all the machine work there. This project took Joe all summer, but he had a lot of fun.

Pop helped Joe put it all back together, and then they attempted to start it up. I remember standing there as the engine turned over a few times and bristled back to life. I remember it because Joe and Pop became ecstatic. They started jumping up and down like they had just won a million dollars. But the old gal was still not road worthy. Joe's good friend, Richard McLane, had come over from Gig Harbor and he was showing Rick how cool this engine was. Joe said that he "was bent over the hood, manually yanking on the throttle linkage because this is what he had seen other mechanics do and thought that imitating other mechanics must be a good thing to do. Then all of a sudden on about my fourth or fifth yank on the throttle linkage, I heard a loud BANG! And the whole engine went into a terrible shudder. Something had happened. Something VERY BIG!! I didn't know what happened, so I just shut down the engine to look. Everything looked okay, so Rich and I decided to start it again. It started right up, but had a bad shake to it. When I revved the engine up, it shuddered violently, so I shut it back down AGAIN.

I looked and looked and couldn't discover anything wrong. I thought that I had thrown a rod, but doing a compression check showed everything was okay. I looked some more, but nothing. I looked at the distributor and it was fine. I looked at the water pump, the generator (Yes, generator. In those days they were generators, not alternators). I looked at the starter, still nothing. I couldn't see what was causing the wild vibrations. I started walking around the truck, just kind of running my hand along the side and literally scratching my head when I was near the front right side of the truck and noticed a hole or slice in the side. It was about 10 inches long from top to bottom with sharp edges and the paint was cracking, so I could tell it was brand new. How did a 10-inch slice in the side of my truck happen? Then I noticed something really peculiar. The sharp edges were facing out as if something from inside the engine had been thrown out. I crawled up onto the front bumper (this was when it still had a front bumper) and peered inside. You wouldn't believe what I found.

One of the fan blades of my cooling fan had broken off and went horizontally right through the side of the truck. The heavy steel fan was NOW out of balance which was causing the engine to violently shake. But what's worse or should I say lucky for me, the blade went out horizontally and not vertically. When the blade let loose, I was leaning over the engine from the front across where the fan was. Had the blade let loose another 95 degrees or so further in its rotation, that 10-inch slice in the side of the Bomb would have gone right through me. My abdomen would have had a ten inch hole. I told both Grandpa Ben and Pop what had happened. They didn't seem to think it was that big of a deal. I knew better. From that day forward, if I ever wanted to impress someone and yank on a throttle linkage to make the engine go 'Varoom, Varoom' I always stood off to the side, away from where the blade parts would shoot out of the side of the vehicle. AND… for anyone reading this, I don't trust the plastic ones (UHMW blades) any more than the heavy duty metal ones. They would make just as neat and clean of a hole through a person. I looked for days, weeks, and years for that blade. Never did find it. For all I know, it may still be out in Farmer Browne's field. Let me stop here to emphasize how powerful the fin was. The metal on those old trucks were VERY thick and that blade sliced it like butter.

So, the truck being done, Joe insisted on running it with or without the fan blade. So Joe took all the blades off until he could get a new one with a bolt pattern that would match up with a six bladed fan. This allowed the engine to run without a vibration, but without a cooling fan. Butchy (Joe's nickname) discovered that he couldn't just take another fan off just any car, since the new cars were all four bladed. Joe's truck was a six and no bolt patterns would match up.

With the engine project complete, Joe started in on the rest. New tie rods, wheels and temperature gauge were added. Well, the old temperature gauge went right into the engine block and Joe broke the gauge right off. He couldn't find a new one, so Joe improvised. He got a hold of a used temperature gauge that would fit into the block and using electrician tape fastened it under the dash. Joe knew he could go quarter mile down the driveway and quarter mile back without the engine overheating, so that's what he did. Everyday Joe would run that truck to the end of the driveway and back just to get the mail. As you know, Mom is very sharp and figured it out right away. While cooking dinner one evening she said to me, "You know Joe, we only get mail once a day and never on Sunday. You don't really have to go out to the mailbox three or four times a day, even on Sunday to check the mail."

I think Mr. Ryan finally gave Joe a fan blade he had laying around at his garage (don't know who told him I needed a new fan; it could have been Pop, but I suspect Mom called him to ask). Mr. Ryan was a family friend who owned the Exxon station at Olympic Village.

Joe lined the "new" fan up and the bolts fit perfectly. First order of business, seats for the back. Joe ran up to the dump (referred to as sanitary landfills now) just a mile from our home and found the best sofa in the lot.

In those days people set good items alongside the driveway at the dump. This was better than recycling, it was reusing. Joe picked up the best two couches for that truck. They fit PERFECTLY in the back from behind the passenger and driver seats to the back door. And when you closed the door, there was about a half inch gap. It was as if the sofas were made for that truck. It worked really well unless you didn't balance the weight. If everyone sat on one side, it made the truck a little hard to handle. Actually, it was very hard to handle. However it really only shows up when you're going 60 or 70 down the freeway."

RUNNING AWAY
1967

Sure it was a dumb idea...to run away from home. But in 1960, my seven year old brother, John, combined with my four year old brain made us think the world revolved around us. This is much like human who think they don't need God to direct their life. I am still unsure why John and I were upset, but pretty sure we didn't get our way on something. So we started planning to run away from home.

"The first thing we need to do," my seven year old brother told me, "is to look at the sun so we can store up the light in our eyes. That way we can see any cliffs at night and not fall off them." As we packed our backpacks, we put in rope so we could climb down any cliffs we came to. Mom made us sandwiches, so we would have something to eat. We added a flashlight and an extra change of clothes.

I went to Mom to say goodbye. She gave us a hug, and said, "I am going to be so sad and miss you A LOT." She had those sad puppy dog eyes as she said goodbye. Well, that did it!! I didn't want Mom to be sad, so I told John that I wasn't going to run away.

John said, "Okay, well, if you don't go who will hold the rope for me to lower myself down the cliffs...I guess I can't go either." Mom pretended to be so relieved, gave both of us a BIG hug, and thanked us for staying home.

There were some unintended consequences from our actions. Do you remember when I said, "We looked at the sun to store up light?" Well, John had much more will power than I and was able to look at the sun much longer. From that day forward John has had to wear some pretty intense glasses. Fact is, as a teen I discovered that when fighting, all you had to do was knock his glasses off and he was blind as a bat. Still couldn't beat him though...he has VERY long arms and has extraordinary strength.

I have also discovered that when I accidently hurt someone, I shut down and leave (or run)! Grandchildren, examine yourself and see if you do the same thing.

Well, the second and last time I ran away from home was in 1967. Our Fox Island home was snuggled into the hillside with a daylight basement. The front door opened at the upper side of the hill which leveled off onto the lawn. By the way, the front yard was also the top of a 30 – 60 foot cliff and which sported a view like no other (almost 180 deg.). We could see the Narrows Bridge all the way down to Nisqually Flats. We could view the sun rising over Mount Rainier…we could see Mount Saint Helens, and Mount Adams too…BUT I digress.

So, there I was pushing Laura around in her wheelchair in the front lawn before going around the corner. Looking past the house and down the hill I could see Mom working away in our very large vegetable garden. It was then I came up with the greatest idea…I'll push the wheelchair down the hill and grab it at the bottom just in time…just before it goes airborne and lands in the garden….I will be the hero!

I gave the chair a little push and it quickly picked up speed as it went speeding down the hill. I was pretty fast for a 10 year old and simply ducked down between the handles and ran along with it. I guess it would have been a good idea if I had first told Laura what I was doing, since she screamed like I had never heard before. Mom's head popped up from around the rows of vegetables to witness Laura, in her wheelchair flying down the hill, heading straight towards her! She jumped up and ran towards Laura and her wheelchair…there was no way she would make it in time, but NOT me. I popped my head up from behind the chair, grabbed the handles and dug my shoes into the hard ground. It dragged me over 15 feet before sliding to a stop perched over the small three foot barrier. I yelled, "I am a hero!" Mom was very quickly on her way towards me with an angry look on her face.

She yelled, "OH NO, YOU'RE NOT!!" I just knew I was in trouble when Mom slipped in a hole, twisted and fell, breaking her ankle. I quickly ran off…knowing I had just hurt Mom. I didn't think about the fact that I had just left Mom in the garden with a broken ankle and Laura stranded in her wheel chair crying…I think that whole scenario scrambled my 10 year old brain. I couldn't handle all the people I hurt. So, I shut down and ran away from home.

There was one problem…it's very hard to run away from home when living on an island. My brother, Joe, got Mom in the car and they drove to the Fox Island Bridge where they waited for me. As I appeared Mom said, "Get in the car, you're taking me to the hospital." So I got in the car. I think Mom knew me more than anyone else, including myself. She had the right words to calm my confusion and allow me to think clearly again.

During my entire growing up years, I could ALWAYS talk with Mom! She knew when to listen, when to advise, when to just hug me. It was my mother who was my best friend while I was in high school, even though I never put that into words. When it came time to ask my, now bride, for her hand in marriage, it was my mother who I asked advice from. I remember it very clearly. I was milking one of my cows and Mom was busy preparing the next one, when I started asking her about marriage. Other times I wished I had asked for her advice…like when I really liked this one girl in high school, so I walked nearly 20 miles to give her my small barrel cactus and a stick stuck in a can of concrete (so she could use it to tie up any house plants). I didn't even know if she had any house plants, but I had grown up with house plants ALL OVER THE PLACE. My grandmother grew them and my mother grew them. I thought everyone had a lot of house plants…but I was wrong.

SMUGGLER'S COVE
1967

The beach would look very different after every storm hit Fox Island. As a child I remember walking down the high tide mark gawking at all the treasures. On this particular day in 1967, I found a row boat paddle. Further down the beach I discovered a very old pram (a small dingy with a flat bow and stern). At first I thought part of the pram was missing, but soon discovered it was just buried in the sand/gravel on the high tide mark. The boat was so battered that it caused me to wonder if it would even float. After digging it out and pounding (with a rock) a few screws back in place, I tested it out. It leaked; it leaked very badly!

A little farther down the beach I found the other paddle. I then carried the six foot, dripping wet boat, all the way back up the hill to our home to perform more repairs. I would love to say it didn't leak and floated like a swan above the water. But we were very poor and I didn't have any fiberglass or resin, so it was glue and screws. The boat leaked and it floated on the water like a submarine in the process of submerging. I figured out that it would float if I bailed fast enough.

I thought the best place to store my new pram was Smuggler's Cove, right where the stream met the bay. No one lived there, but we knew the people renting the "Dump Chateau" just up the hill (named because they used the location of the dump to explain to friends how to find their home… "first driveway past the dump."). Besides, the water there was ALWAYS smooth, hence no waves would break her apart.

I was so excited to finally have a boat that I called all my Fox Island friends, Gary Lanphere and Mark Miller. We all rode our bikes and met at Smuggler's Cove. It was Gary that wanted to row it from one side to the other and test it out. I told him that he needed someone to bail while he rowed. I didn't want to leave Mark by himself, so I volunteered him to do the bailing. I would swim alongside to make sure they were okay and would be ready just in case the boat went under. I was thinking… "I didn't want them to drown, even though both of them were better swimmers."

Gary and Mark took off across the cove. I could hear their cadence, "stroke, bail, stroke, bail, stroke, bail"…as they worked their way across. I quickly grabbed my buck knife and cut the legs off my pants, then dove in…well, it was more of a run and splash in. I thought I would quickly catch up with them and swim alongside to keep them safe. I was in the very center of Smuggler's Cove when it happened! A cramp hit my right leg! I NEVER had a cramp before and didn't know what happened.

Mark and Gary were about 15 – 20 feet in front when I started struggling. Mark was first to notice and yelled, "GARY, BACK, DANIEL'S GOT A CRAMP!" I was bobbing, sputtering, and coughing as I struggled to keep my head above water. Gary quickly put the oars in reverse and started rowing in my direction. By the time they got to me I was already sinking down, down, down. Mark reached into the water and grabbed me. At that moment our wrists clamped so tightly I don't think anything could have separated us as he pulled me back up. I held on to the side of the boat as Gary put all his strength into rowing us back to the beach.

The extra weight of me holding onto the fragile boat caused the stern to slowly pull away. So when we finally made it to safety, it had nearly come all the way off. After making it to the beach, we pushed the boat back into the cove and watched as it sunk down to the water level and kind of stayed there. That was it! We were safe, the boat was dead, and we all went back home to never mention our adventure again. I didn't even tell my mother about the day Mark Miller and Gary Lamphere saved my life. It would have only caused her more fear about raising an active boy.
Side note: After bringing my pant legs back home, I asked Mom to sew a zipper on them. Then next time I could simply unzip the pant legs and it would be easier than cutting them every time I went swimming. I didn't know 40 years later it would become a new clothing line. LOL

QUICK, MARK IS DROWNING
1967

Mark's eyes screamed trouble as he coughed, took a breath, went under again, arms thrashing about. Something had him by the foot and kept pulling him under. That summer we had gone on field trips with the PLU (Pacific Lutheran University) biology class that my dad was taking. The adults had split up and gone all around the lake collecting specimens in little glass containers. Pop was in a thicket of cattails collecting some swamp insects. Mark and I were swimming out to the small boggy island in the center. It was fun being able to help Pop in his class, collecting and discovering different plant and animal life in the swamps and lakes of Washington State.

Just one week before we were collecting specimens during low tide by Point Defiance. I just can't describe the excitement I felt collecting marine invertebrates from the bay. Many years before my mother had given me a book which became by far my favorite. It was a book with the photos of all the marine invertebrates of Puget Sound. I must have looked and studied each and every photo a billion times and memorized each animal by name. As the class went from one rock to the next, the professor would ask the students, "What is that animal?" It was exciting because if no one knew, he would allow me to answer and I always got it right. I was like most boys and ate up all encouragement from adults for breakfast, lunch and dinner.

It reminds me of the time when I was in high school and I was working down at the Peninsula High School Marine Lab with the teacher, George. He was the best teacher I had ever had and many times he and I would go to the beach to collect animals for the aquariums. One day we happened to come across a class from UPS (University of Puget Sound). George whispered to me to go over by them and collect a few animals. I knew what he was doing, so I moseyed closer and the professor was doing the same thing, asking the students what this and that animal were. I think I frustrated the adults and professor because I kept giving the correct answer when they didn't know. But I wouldn't just give the common name I would also add the genus and species of the animal. Being a high school student I wasn't supposed to know more than college students (or the professor) in their marine biology. My teacher got his Master's Degree studying marine biology at UPS and had this same professor. Later George told me that the professor and he had locked horns when he was a college student. It felt good to him and me that his high school student outperformed the professor's marine biology students.

A year before, my dad took the entire family to Westport for a camping vacation with the ham radio club. I was excited about going down to the docks, laying on my stomach, and peering in the water. So many animals lived on the bottom of the platoons; I would be entertained for hours. One problem with having younger siblings is that they want to do what the big boys do and will follow you around. I hadn't noticed that four year old Tom had followed me down to the docks. I remember a couple of older boys were fishing, but didn't give them any mind since I was there to look at all the animals. While laying there transfixed with the sea life I heard a, "SPLASH" which shocked me out of the trance. Looking up, I noticed my brother splashing in the water. I quickly grabbed one of the fishing poles right out of the older boy's hands, stretched it out until Tom could grab the tip and pulled him in. That was the day I saved my brother, Tom's life.

Oh, I almost forgot about Mark. His foot was caught in the roots of the lily pad (Rhizoids). As the roots grew for many years they intertwined with each other creating a root mat. If you pulled up on the roots the mat would pull you right back down and Mark's foot was caught in that mat. I quickly looked around for a long stick, but couldn't find anything. There wasn't anything I could throw to him either. I remember in Boy Scouts they always said, "Reach, throw, go." However, they always cautioned us that to go out there to save someone would put your own life at risk. I was taught that the drowning person will surely pull you down in panic. I only had a split second to think, so I didn't. I was not a great swimmer and as I swam towards my best friend, I knew he would pull me under. As soon as I reached him, I took a very deep breath and sure enough Mark latched onto me and I went under. I pushed on the mat, hoping it would free his foot. The force of me going under and Mark pulling up allowed his foot to become free of the twisted roots and Mark let go of me as we swam back to the dock.

I had forgotten about the story of saving Mark's life and Mark had forgotten the story about Smuggler's Cove where he saved my life. It was over fifty years before we ever talked about it again and reminded each other of how we saved each other's lives. I guess that's how it works with friends.

OUR SCHOOL BUS LOST IT'S BRAKES
1967

As an elementary age child (I think I was in fifth grade) I used to visit with a friend named Marty Ketcham. He was my neighbor...well, back then your neighbor could have lived a couple miles away, as in this case. I would yell to Mom and say, "I'm going over to Marty's house."

She would reply, "Okay, be back before the lights come on the bridge (Narrows Bridge)." I always thought it was strange, since most places on the island I couldn't see the lights if they were on or off. Maybe she meant before dark. I'd show up and Marty would ask his mother if we could go swimming. If she said yes, I would take my pocket knife and cut my pants into cut-offs (shorts). Well, I was not that good of a swimmer and I think Marty's mother knew it so she always insisted that everyone wear life jackets. She had the largest life jackets I had ever seen. Many times the tide would be just right (almost all the way in) and we'd swim for hours with those very large life jackets (they also kept us warm). When I got home I would ask Mom to sew the legs back on my pants...she only did it a couple times and from then on I was not allowed to make shorts out of my pants. This is when the idea of putting a zipper on the legs surfaced, so I could take them off or on anytime I needed to. Now there is a clothing line that used the same concept...I see people wearing them all the time.

Marty also had a dog that would follow him to the bus stop. After we got on, it would chase the bus up the hill on Mowitch Drive. All the kids would open the windows and yell out encouragement to Old Blue...He was the fastest dog on the island AND the fastest dog we had ever seen (greyhound). The bus driver would yell out how fast Blue was going as he picked up speed. It was a different time...when an 11 yr old would go miles away from home to go play/swim and come back just as it was getting dark. Surprisingly, the bus driver would shout encouragement to a dog running alongside his bus. By the time I was in seventh grade I would head out into the woods just to get lost. I discovered A LOT of places and things. (I'll tell you about my discoveries in separate story) I would let Mom know that, "If I am not back before dark don't worry, I am probably lost in the woods." Then I would tell her, "If I'm not back by 9:00 A.M. THEN you can worry and send a search party." I did get lost several times, and stayed the night a few times...and caught fish without a pole or hand line so I would have something to eat while "lost."

Back then the substitute bus driver was also the mechanic. On this particular day, the mechanic worked furiously to get the bus ready to drop off children. I think the Lord was watching over us, since it was also the mechanic who was driving when the brakes went out.

We had already dropped of Gary Lamphere, then come off the bulkhead road by the Milton's place, up the hill past where the new store is now, then turned left past the post office and down the steep hill. That's when I noticed the driver pumping the brakes.

I knew what that meant since I remembered in 1964 when Mom and Pop were driving us across the Rocky Mountains and the brakes went out. Since Pop was driving the truck with our large camping trailer, Mom was driving the station wagon with a smaller trailer. She had us children praying as she called Pop on the ham radio and he walked her through her options on how to stop a car without brakes. She pumped the brakes until she got enough pressure to slow the car and trailer, but we still couldn't stop. So she devised a plan to have Joe and Tim (12 and 10.5 years) jump out of the car, grab a rock and shove it under the wheels. As we were going down the steep hill and before she could slow enough, we saw a gravel parking lot. Mom aimed for the lot, put our station wagon and trailer into a power slide, pulled the parking brake, and spun 180 degrees. My older brothers yelled, "YEEHAW!" We were really proud of Mom and felt even more secure knowing she was in control.

Okay, back to the school bus with no brakes. The bus rocketed down the hill past the post office, then started up the next. The driver shifted down, which allowed us to slow enough to make the next turn onto Adams Lane. Keeping it in a lower gear, he turned the next corner (7th Lane), slowed more, and had my friend, Cindy, jump out. Then he shifted to pick up speed until the next stop. By the time he got to our drop off point, we all knew the routine. This was one of the only times that Mom was at our stop waiting for us to get off the bus. He was able to get the bus to slow down to walking speed…well a fast walking speed. He opened the door and one by one we started hopping off. Mom thought it was strange that the bus didn't stop, so she asked us what we did wrong to make it so the driver didn't stop. We told her that the brakes went out, so he could only slow down to let us off. Mom didn't seem concerned, so neither were we. After all, it was 1968 and things like this just happened.

I FOUND A LARGE DIAMOND
1968

I think I was in fifth grade when I found a VERY LARGE diamond. It seemed like I just lived on the beach and most of the time my sister, Mary, and I were on our hands and knees crawling along the high tide mark meticulously search for treasures. Hour after hour, we would crawl along picking up small quarter inch shells and the skeletons of the small shore crabs. When we had enough small shells to fill two baby food jars we sold them. Pop packed us into the station wagon and off to the city we went. The word excitement did not describe well enough how we felt.

Mary and I took our shells and crab skeletons into the Day Island gift shop and left with 50 cents. Our disappointment was thick! We couldn't believe that for hours we would pick up shells that they wanted and we only got 50 cents. Pop turned to us and asked a very simple question, "What did you learn from this experience?" He too seemed a little disappointed, not in us, but that we were paid 50 cents after all our effort.

Sure there's a lesson here, but this is not the total story. While we were collecting shells, I came upon a two inch diamond. Sometimes I would rake the pebbles with my fingers to stir up a few more shells. It so happened, that on one of these "pebble stirs" a diamond popped right up and onto the surface.

The next day at school was my turn for show and tell. I was planning to bring a cigar box with my insect collection, but with the discovery of the diamond I decided to bring it along too. One disadvantage of being from a very large family is from time to time you don't get access to adult advice. If I had shown my mother or father, they would have advised me to keep it home. Then we would have gone to a jewelry store and had it professionally identified, but I didn't and now it was too late.

Things went very well, as I showed my insect collection to the class and then I presented the diamond. Mr. Dugay was very impressed and asked if we could test it to see if it was real. Well, he couldn't tell, but most the children were more impressed with the insect collection than the rock.

What a neat day at school! On my long bus ride home all the children loved seeing the insect collection and diamond. Then there was this one girl; I really can't remember her name. She was new this year to the island and moved soon after, but boy oh boy she was VERY pretty. Her hair was ALWAYS brushed perfectly with long curls, her nose was also perfectly formed; she was very girly. She never talked to me or even looked my way and I always thought she was a bit stuck up. But then it happened, she came over and sat with me on the bus! I couldn't believe this was happening! It was like beauty and the beast! She batted her eyelashes at me and said, "Daniel, that is such a great bug collection, do you think I can take it home to show my mother?"

I was putty in her hands. "Oh, of course, just bring it back tomorrow," I said.

The next day she sat in a seat far away. I called to her and asked if she brought my insect collection back. "Oh, yes, I almost forgot, thank you Daniel" she replied as she handed it to the person behind her to pass it back to me.

I opened up the box and noticed my diamond was missing. So I asked her, "Where's my diamond?"

She replied, "You must have taken it out before you handed me the box. I only wanted to show my mom the bug collection, remember?"

I thought to myself, "That's right, she only asked to borrow the 'bug' collection, not the diamond, BUT I remember keeping them together in the box." From that day forward I learned a VERY valuable life lesson. Some girls are pretty on the outside, BUT very devious and ugly on the inside. I felt very bad and never told my mom or dad about what had happened. I knew she stole my diamond and I would never get it back and I never did.

FRIENDS
1968

It's very important that you are careful who you hang out with. I was blessed with a large family and a dad that kept drilling into us, "Don't do ANYTHING that will tarnish the family name!" This is what was echoing though my head whenever I was with TJ. He didn't last long on the island and I was quite relieved.

One day TJ broke into the museum archives at the Fox Island School. He stole a WWI jumpsuit, took it to Smuggler's Cove, stuffed it with straw, then proceeded to beat it up all the while yelling, "TAKE THAT OLD MAN!" There was only one person living on the other side and he looked concerned. I simply watched the entire episode, but didn't think it was right. Something inside me kept saying, "That's not right."

TJ really didn't like playing with me, especially when some of my other friends were around. When TJ would say something to do that wasn't right I would say, "NO! That's not a nice thing to do!!" Or, "Go ahead, but I am not having anything to do with it!"

He would say out loud and in front of me, "Let's not play with Daniel, he takes the fun out of things." Well, really I just never wanted to get into trouble. What's wrong with that?

On another time the three of us were riding our bikes when TJ came up with the idea of ditching me. Of course I wasn't let in on the secret, as only my friend and TJ knew. He said, "Let's go down this trail," so we headed down, with TJ first, then my friend, then me. I didn't know that trail too well, so I started lagging behind when it happened. TJ slid his bike behind a tree, then my friend hid, and I kept riding right past them without knowing. Coming to the end of the trail I could tell I was ditched, so I went home. About an hour or so I got a call from my friend's mom who asked where I was. I told her I was at home and that TJ and her son had ditched me. She asked why and I said, "I don't know." She then asked me how long I had been at home and I told her, "A couple hours."

Evidently TJ got the idea of robbing a house and knew I would ruin his fun. However, he got caught by the owner, along with my friend. TJ quickly made up a story to the home owner that I was the one that broke into the home and that he was just there to find me and stop me. The owner called my friend's mom and she called me to ask for my side of the story. She then sat her son down and forced the truth out of him.

From that day on my one friend was not allowed to play with TJ, but was allowed to play with me. TJ's mom wouldn't let TJ play with me, "since I got her son in trouble." She believed him!

I think on that day I became more of an introvert and it was then I discovered how fun work was rather than playing with my friends. Slowly, I discovered hanging out with adults was safer and more fun than with kids my own age. This manifested and followed me all the way through high school where upon in 1979 I got married. The groomsmen included, my science teacher (George Palo), my English teacher, (Kevin Miller) and my shop/construction teacher (Paul Wise). They were all like good mentors and brothers to me. After ninth grade when my friends attended keggers, I'd just as soon be home or at George's house, or sanding George's sailboat, or working on Paul's new home. I always said, "I like hanging out with the adults as they don't do stupid things."

I HURT A GIRL
1968

When we were in sixth grade the teachers took us on a field trip to Vashon Island. I have NO clue why we went there, but we did. We rode the bus to the ferry, then rode the ferry to a park on the island, played at the park, and ate our lunches.

I had a big crush on a beautiful girl with long, brown hair, and a smile that could reach all the way around you, and a laugh that made the sun shine...The girl liked a boy named Ty. Being a sixth grade boy, I had a hard time understanding these new feelings...I was really wrestling with what it all meant. Well, to show her that I liked her, I threw a pop can and it hit her in the head. Blood came pouring down her beautiful face and across her lips. I ran and hid until the ferry came to take us home. I ran onto the ferry then snuck back in the school bus and just stayed. At one point a girl named Loren must have known something was wrong, so she sat with me and started talking (girls have such an advantage with understanding of their own and other's feelings). She got me to start smiling, but when I finally looked up I saw one of the teachers scowling at me...I quickly shut back down. We got off the bus at Artondale and instead of riding our bus home, I ran into the woods and hid. I watched and waited for all the buses to leave, then started my trek home crying all the way. As I was passing the Fox Island cemetery the driver of the high school bus pulled up next to me, stopped the bus, opened the door, and told me to get in. So I rode the rest of the way home.

At home, being around seven other boys, I was very careful not to say anything about what happened. I was too hurt to even tell my best friend, who happened to be my sister. The next day I went to school and pretended that nothing happened. Mrs. Wolfram called me out into the hallway to talk with me. She said, "Daniel, why did you miss the bus yesterday?" I burst out crying and couldn't stop. I told her that I didn't mean to hurt Terri, but I felt better after telling someone.

Even to this day I have a VERY hard time dealing with internal pain when I accidently hurt someone. I have also noticed that many of my grandsons do the exact same thing. When they do something wrong, hurts someone, or just makes someone mad at them they run, hide, and or shut down. Reminds me a lot about Adam and Eve's response to what they did: ran, hid, and shut down.

Two other lessons from this was how I felt when I discovered a feeling that I had NEVER felt before. I liked that pretty girl and I had never had feelings like that before. To express my feelings I threw a pop can at her because I just didn't know how to get my arms around these new feelings. It seems girls are always exploring feelings, talking about them, and thinking through them.

I felt much better talking to someone who I respected about my feelings. I wish I had told my sister, (she's real smart) but at least my teacher figured it out and helped me work through the pain I was feeling and the pain I caused.

STUCK IN A BARBWIRE FENCE
1968

I don't know what I would have done without my bicycle. At first I rode a three speed bicycle all over the island. By the time I got a TEN speed I made a goal to ride up, without stopping, EVERY road and every hill the island had no matter how steep. It was easier to ride up the steep hills in the 60's for there were very few cars, so what I did was use the width of the road as switchbacks. The island was also VERY quiet, so if a car was coming I could hear it miles away, which gave me time to get back to my side of the road or stop, then go back down and start again. The toughest hill was Kamas, not the main hill, but the one going east up from the beach. I guess someone re-named that part Rainier.

Before I got my three speed bike, I had a regular small, one speed bike that I rode to Mark Miller's, Gary Lamphere's or to Arletta to visit John Ford. One year Gary moved to 12th Avenue at the bottom of the hill. I could ride there in minutes, since he was so much closer. There was a driveway that was called, "Lover's Lane," which made my trek much shorter. I would start riding up Mowitch, past 13th Ave., down the dip and start up the hill. There was a driveway on the right, just as you started up the hill. That horseshoe driveway skirted the big hill and allowed me to ride from Mowitch to 12th Avenue without much effort. I just LOVED that shortcut because the driveway started out going downhill and with a full head of speed you could make it to 12th Avenue without much peddling. Although there were two houses accessing the road, no one lived down there except "summer people."

One day I headed over to Gary's house by way of Lover's Lane. It was just awesome, as I took off down that horseshoe road at full speed, up and down small hills, around blind corners. I was really going fast, but then it happened! I rounded one of the last blind corners and WHAM, I ran right into four strands of barbed wire that were stretched across the road. My bike hit the fence and disappeared. My head went between the strands, but the rest of my body somehow zipped or rolled around the barbed wire. I was stuck, just suspended in the air, lying perpendicular to the road. I didn't feel hurt, but I couldn't move because the wire was so tightly wrapped around my legs, arms and body. Did I mention that before I hit the fence I was really moving fast?

I don't know how long I was incapacitated, but I did finally free up my right hand that I used to free one of my arms. Then I was able to pull both arms out and untangle my legs and head. I found my bike and started out again, much slower this time. On my way out I noticed a sign that said, "No Trespassing" near a summer person's house and on the driveway. You could only read the sign if you were coming from 12th Ave. I guess they didn't want me to use this shortcut anymore. From that day on I took the long way to Gary's house. Of course I thought I'd be in trouble if I ever told my parents since I was trespassing down that driveway. To this day I don't know why they didn't want me to ride my bike down their driveway…maybe they just didn't want cars to go down it?

About a month later, somewhere near Gig Harbor, a boy kept riding his motorcycle through someone's woods. The owner became upset and strung a strand of barbwire across the trail in order to stop him from trespassing. That wire seriously injured the boy which made me even more hesitant of telling my parents about this event. I was really afraid I'd get in trouble.

GOING SKIING
1969

My brothers, Joe and Tim were good at everything they put their hands on. I remember when the Olympics were on TV and Joe, Tim and Dan wanted skis, so they could practice for the Olympics. We were downright poor and couldn't go on the school ski trip AND couldn't afford to rent skis, so Joe decided to make our own. We went down to the carpenter shop and secured a three foot wooden barrel. After taking off the metal straps, we sanded two slats each, and lacquered them. Then using wood screws we anchored a WWII army boot on each slat and waxed them with bar soap.

Next we went out to an old logging road to gather small alder saplings which would be used for ski poles. Now the only thing needed was snow... we waited, and waited, and waited. One of the downfalls of living down close to the bay is that the water keeps the air warmer than the top of the island. I remember in 1970 when school was closed because of snow. We just couldn't figure out why, until we drove to the top of the island and discovered over TWO feet of snow. We only had a dusting.

Finally, Joe and Tim said, "We can't be sitting around here waiting; we need to go to Snoqualmie Pass where they train for skiing in the Olympics." He also explained that when you're skiing you exert a lot of energy, so you don't want to wear too heavy of clothing, just wear cut offs. So before throwing their "skis" and alder sticks (poles) into the back of the pick-up, we cut off our pant legs so we wouldn't become overheated during a day of skiing.

Years later, I met many avid skiers and what I noticed most is that they were constantly "evaluating" other skiers. "Would you look at those hicks, they don't even know which way to put their skis on their car."

Another line I heard was, "Look, they are leaning their skis against their car, what idiots!"

Another time I heard one say, "Can you believe that outfit? Who goes skiing with that on, how embarrassing!"

Well, needless to say after my brother's and my arrival at Snoqualmie Pass Ski Resort the entire hillside was abuzz with gossip. I didn't notice and we really didn't care because we were preparing for the next Olympics.

As we strutted up the path, sporting our cutoffs and army boots, with homemade skis under one arm and alder saplings under the other, I noticed a sign. It read, 'Skiing lessons.' I said to Joe and Tim, "We don't have any money for lessons, so let's sneak into the class. We'll just go up next to that guy and blend in." Well, blending in didn't really work; we were quickly discovered and moved out. I was very persistent though, so I tried another tactic that worked. I found a large discarded cup, used my buck knife and cut the bottom out, and by putting it to my ear I could get close enough not to be discovered, but could hear the instructor. Being very sneaky, I got closer and closer until I could see and hear everything the instructor was demonstrating.

I relayed the information to my brothers. "When you point the tips of the skis together it is called snowplowing and you can stop. On steeper hills you put your weight on the upper ski and go perpendicular to the hill, flip and go the other way." I looked over at Tim and Joe then said, "I got it, this is going to be easy; let's go to the top and try it." So up we went to the top of the tallest hill. As I got to the top I said to myself, "THAT IS NOT A HILL, IT IS A CLIFF AND PEOPLE ARE GOING OVER THE EDGE!" I watched as one after the other would disappear over the edge. I just couldn't believe my eyes, and neither did Tim or Joe who quickly rode the lift back down. However, I wasn't going to give up that easy. So I inched my way to the edge and peered over. They weren't falling at all, they were going perpendicular to the hill, just as that ski instructor demonstrated. So, I decided that if I wanted to be in the Olympics, I better watch and learn.

After about a half hour someone said, "Are you going to go?" So I went. I dug my left ski into the edge of the cliff and it worked, I slid all the way to the other side. I fell down, turned around, and dug my right ski into the side of the cliff and away I went to the other side.

I did this for nearly an hour and wasn't even 10 feet down the hill. When I looked over my shoulder, I could still see where I had started. "THIS WAS NOT WORKING!" Out of frustration, out of patience, and out of my mind I decided to GO FOR IT! After all, I saw how the Olympians skied down the slopes between those sticks with flags on them.

"If they could do it, so could I!" And away I went, tucking those poles under each arm, squatting down, putting my skis together, and down the cliff/hill I went. "I must have been going 200 mile per hour!!! I wasn't scared, well, maybe a little, but what I most worried about was all the people skiing back and forth that were in my path. I was so worried I would hurt one of them. So I let out a warning holding my poles into the air waving them back and forth and yelling, "LOOK OUT BELOW!" as I flew past each one at 300 mph. Thank goodness at the bottom of the slopes they had a large pile of snow for people to run into and stop.

Tim described it differently. "Well, when Joe I saw the cliff we said to ourselves, "our momma didn't raise no fool, so we decided to ride the lift back down." After all, I paid for the ride and I just wanted my money's worth. After waiting an hour for Dan at the bottom, Joe and I decided to get a coffee and look for girls. Well, at least we got some coffee. I sat down at the outside table and just waited and waited until finally we thought we could see Dan. He was the only one wearing shorts, and his legs were so white they camouflaged with the snowy background. I overheard one person talking about him. He said something like, 'I am glad I wore sunglasses today." Everyone else was wearing some slick type of long pants with suspenders or straps that they just pulled off if they got too warm. Anyway, I saw Dan at the top of the hill going back and forth, back and forth. I think some people passed him two or three times. They would come down the hill ride the lift back up and pass him again. Then it happened. I don't know what got into him, but he came screaming down the hill at full speed. I think he was going 400 mph. It seemed as though the second he started down everyone quickly scurried to the sides and watched. After he hit the snow bank at the bottom everyone cheered. Dan thought they were cheering because he was ready for the Olympics, but I don't think so.

The next winter Joe came up with a better idea. "We're going to ski at Hurricane Ridge (in the Olympic Mountains). It's closer than Snoqualmie and I can actually ski in the Olympics."

Family members FB comments:

Joe Bushnell: Yes, they were barrel slats. I took a short barrel and used three slats to make one pair. Two slats were used to make the skies. One slat was cut in half to make the bindings. With some experimenting around on mud going down the small hill on the south side of the house, I found the best position to mount the bindings was all the way to the back. I sanded the bottom side to a fine finish and used a poly finish that I sanded out with a 100 grit sand paper to a fine finish. For ski wax, I used dial soap. It worked great except the skis had a tendency to go down the hill sideways.

Timothy Bushnell: Tim H was there, laughing his tail off for us to stop. I would spin left, get dizzy & fall over. Then I spun right & fell over, ran into one of my compadres or not and we both would fall over. Fun was an understatement. I was "kicked off" the rope lift; I had no tips, ski digs in feet stop, BUT I stayed ahold of the rope and was drug up the hill on my behind. GREAT FUN!

Diana Bushnell: Tim told me that a man questioned him about the short skis, how easy they were to maneuver, etc. Tim was really flattered by the attention. Shortly after that a line of short skis were on the market.

Timothy Bushnell: True, he spoke w/ a German or Swiss accent. He reminisced about how he had barrel skis as a child. The next year "King Headway" short skis for learning was quite popular.

Lawrence D. Bushnell: I remember shortly after Joe and Tim had their adventure with the barrel skies, the new rave on the slopes were short skies. .... just saying.

BROKEN DOWN ON THE NARROWS BRIDGE
1969

We had a bob-tailed cat that was a GREAT mouser. It was dark out so Tim and Mom didn't know Whitey, our white cat, sneaked into the Blue Bomb through a hole in the floor. Tim and Mom had just headed out on that dark, icy, snowy night to driver's education class at Peninsula High School. Tim was heading north on Hwy 16 (before the new bypass which is now called Purdy Drive NW was created). He had turned onto 144th so he could go up around the football field and come down into the back parking lot where Mr. Stoican's driver's education class met. Before heading up the hill onto 144th Mom had him pull into the Chevron Station.

Well, let's have Tim explain: I was going into the gas station and went the "short way." It just so happened that someone put up a "Wrong Way" sign there. The trooper asked me if I saw that sign. I said, "Did it say, Do Not Enter?"

He said, "No, Wrong Way." To my surprise and the trooper's, Whitey jumped onto my lap and out the window. The cat caused the officer a great fright which nearly landed him on his back as his arms flew outward like a humming bird and his feet started sliding back and forth on the icy road. After knocking the officer's hat off and running once around his shoulders it turned and headed into the woods. He helped us look and look for Whitey, but to no avail. Since I went to school in Tacoma (Bellarmine) he figured I just didn't know my way around very well and he let me off with a warning. It could have been that he just wanted to forget about what had just happened and a ticket could bring back a frightful event.

A year or two later the Blue Bomb broke down in the very middle of the Narrows Bridge. The SAME officer was on scene and he, 'looked very hesitant.' Mom thought he was worried that another cat would jump out at him. So, instead of going to the driver's window he opened the back. It could have been because traffic was very close to the driver's window. Well, anyway, he opened the back door and this time a large goat jumped out. Although he didn't swear, we could tell he thought SOMEONE was pulling a practical joke on him! Who carries a goat around in the back of their car? He kept looking around like there was a hidden camera somewhere on the bridge. We don't usually haul our goats around in the panel truck, but it was needed in a play Tim and Jim Ford were in at Bellarmine High School. It was the most humane way of transporting animals, no wind, kind of "warm" and easy to keep an eye on when you're sitting right next to them.

The officer told us to get in his patrol car to stay warm, but soon became upset when he looked in and saw Elizabeth, the goat, sitting on our laps looking out at him. He yelled, "NO GOATS IN MY PATROL CAR!!" So we all got out and stood in the wind, in the middle of the Narrows Bridge with Elizabeth at our side. We did get some inquisitive looks, but we didn't pay it any mind. If Elizabeth wasn't allowed in the car, no one was going to be in the car. We waited another hour until one of our brothers showed up with the family station wagon, where everyone was welcome, even the goat. We made it to the play in time for Elizabeth, Tim and Jim to do their part.

This event caused me to pause and think…were we like hillbillies to everyone else? Oh well, who cares? It was fun growing up with 10 siblings while living on an island. I've been told Fox Island is very much different and so am I…well a little bit anyway.

SURVIVAL TRAINING GONE "WRONG"
1970

Fox Island had a Boy Scout camp donated by Colonel Nichols over by 11th Ave. It also had one Boy Scout troop, but two patrols. The patrol my brother John belonged to was called the "Kudu patrol." At one point we were sent out for survival training and the best way to learn was to jump in with both feet. That is exactly what our Scout Master, our dad, did. The patrol included John Bushnell (my brother), Happy T., Gary J., Jim F. and Kevin Mc. We were all sent out into the wilderness to survive the elements. All we were allowed to bring was a sleeping bag, a pocket knife, and a survival manual.

Turns out that during this great ordeal, they were given a large chocolate cake from Gary's mother, and more goodies from Mrs. Mc., Mrs. F. put in some cookies, and Mrs. T. and our Mom also donated snacks. To this day Pop had no idea what the ladies had done. We decided that it was okay to take these goodies because we figured that manipulating mothers for food was part of survival techniques for any teenage boy.

Pop's heart was in the right place. He had survived being chased in the jungle for two days and nights after being shot down during WWII. He also took survival training in the Arctic and wrote the manual for search and rescue at its inception.

Pop did teach us how to catch fish without a pole and it really worked. One time, when camping on the west side of the island, by the big rock, I walked out, very slowly into the water until I was chest deep. I turned parallel to the beach and walked until I saw a flounder move between me and the beach. I carefully walked towards the flounder, very slowly. The flounder moved, swam about two feet away, and stopped. Slowly I would take a step or two towards the fish and it moved again. Being very patient I repeated this process until the flounder was only a foot or two away from the shore. Then I started scooping the water like mad and during one of those scoops I flipped the flounder onto the beach.

I hadn't ever made fire without a match, but wish I had. Before camping I always dipped the tips of my matches in candle wax (but not too much wax) so if they got wet I could still make a fire. I took a limb and where it branched off I set the fish. I then took many smaller green twigs and wove them around the fish and branch to make a small fish holder before hovering it above the fire. There's just something about fishing without a pole, cooking without utensils, and becoming full. I did bring a pot to boil and picked stinging nettles to make tea.

It was so peaceful sitting on the beach by the big rock, leaning against the drift wood log, listening to the calm water lapping on shore, the sounds of loons echoing across the bay, and the snapping of the fire. So few people lived on the island back then AND you were allowed to walk on any of the beaches all the way around the island.

BURIED TREASURE
1970

Just for fun in seventh grade I would go into the woods just to get lost. Mom and I had an understanding. I would always tell her before I headed out and she would not worry if I didn't make it back before dark (don't know if she held up her part of the agreement) since I would just sleep where I was.

However, if I didn't make it back before 9:00 the next morning something was wrong…but I always made it back before 9:00. I think only two times I headed out too late in the day and had to spend the night in the woods. I loved the freedom, trust, discoveries and adventure of growing up on Fox Island.

I discovered an old fire truck that had trees growing out of it. It was located…well, if you drove east on Island Blvd. and held your steering wheel tight, go across 9th Ave, and drive through the woods for about 150' you would run right into it. I was so excited about my discovery that I went to the museum (the museum was in the old school house at that time) and told Mr. Miller (Mike Miller's grandpa). He told me the entire history of that old fire truck. I really liked Mr. Miller as he ALWAYS treated everyone with respect and courteously even during my rebellious high school years.

Another time I found an old donkey engine, but this time Mr. Brown told me the story behind it. It was/is located on the southwest side of Island Blvd, just past 11th Ave. and around 150 feet off the road, so deep in the woods that you couldn't see it from the road.

The king of all discoveries was an old one room beach cabin located directly east of our farm and all the way to the other side (width) of the island. The door was stuck open, the window was no longer there (just a large hole), a bunk bed with only springs stood to one side, but the roof was in great shape. Twenty feet away I discovered a fresh water spring. This became my main destination when exploring the woods, camping, or just hanging out. Sure I kept exploring the woods, but if it was rainy I

91

would go directly to the old shelter. It was tucked back behind some trees, but you could still see the bay and McNeil Island.

I would catch sole or flounder by hand, a survival trick my dad taught me years before. After a good meal, I would drink some nettle tea and call it a day. A better description of its location; go to the big rock and walk northwest along the high tide mark for about 500 feet. Look to your right and you should see fresh water coming out of the bank. Climb up the small embankment to the top, then go right (southeast) about 20-40 feet.

The cabin is mainly what I was talking about. If you walked down the beach (yes, away from Steilacoom) until the cliff was only 10 - 15 feet high you will notice the old one room cabin hidden away in the woods. It was about 20 feet to the right (back toward the big rock, but where the cliff is about 15 -20' above the beach...it was easy to walk right past without seeing it. I didn't see it until about the sixth time, but I followed that old trail and did a bit more exploring. There were also two very large logs at this end of that skid road (just an overgrown road in the 60's) that was about 60" wide and 10' long. It looked like the real old timers' were trying to get them to the bay, but for some reason left there.

I did A LOT of climbing of the cliffs... and I remember a very large madrona tree that grew out of the top, its roots exposed to the air. I would climb down the tree trunk to the exposed roots and play, weaving in and out while overhanging the cliff (my mother was glad she didn't know). I also remember a hole in the tree where an owl lived...looking at the owl pellets and seeing all the small shore crab "shells." There was a trail along the top of the cliff from the big rock all the way to the cabin... and trail to the stinging nettles and water spring.

A very old outhouse that was covered with ivy also stood nearby. It was too rotten to go in. I did tell Mr. Browne and his old partner, John, about the cabin and outhouse. They told me that it belonged to a bootlegger and if you dig in the outhouse (which was all dirt by then) you will find a lot of old bottles (considered old in the 1960's). I guess you might say there is some buried treasure on the island. I hope whoever looks for it will be as careful as an archaeologist and donate the bottles to the Fox Island Museum. I know the exact location of the old outhouse, well, back then anyway. Haven't been there since 1979 and suspect it's been built on now.

HANDLING MONEY
1970

Even when I was young I tried to listen to people who had been on the earth longer than I. Many times I received great advice and sometimes the advice only advanced the other person's agenda. Some of the good advice included, "ALWAYS be good to your mother and don't cause her ANY grief." Other good advice came from Mr. Browne or Mom on how to handle money. This last one made things quite awkward for a 10 year old since many of my peers saw things quite differently.

I had a good friend who saved his money for a motorcycle, while I saved mine for a Herford heifer. I figured getting a calf and raising it to become a cow, then breeding her would mean I would have two beef cows. I would then breed those two and I'd have four and so on. However, IF I had used my money on a motorcycle, it would eventually break and cost me money. Just like clockwork sure enough it happened to my friend. On the other hand, he learned to make many repairs on his motorcycle. Both were good learning experiences.

I am not saying it was easy. Instead of playing all the time, I had to build a fence, which meant acquiring cedar and splitting it into posts. It also meant purchasing the fencing, hauling buckets of gravel sometimes a quarter of a mile to each post (the soil had so much clay it wouldn't pack without the beach rocks). By the time I was in middle school I started rebuilding the barn that had nearly collapsed during a snow storm. The ONE time I skipped school was when my dad purchased enough wire so I could run power to the barn. The ditch I dug was nearly 150 feet from the house, half of which went through the very hard driveway.

I had made enough money working at Mr. Browne's that I decided to purchase a milk cow. Then the meat recession hit, gas prices went through the roof, and my dad lost his job as a teacher during the day and custodian in the evening. One day I discovered Pop didn't have enough money for the taxes on the land. The entire summer Pop and I collaborated on how to bring in enough food for the family.

At one point we considered using a fish net to catch a bunch of perch and other fish for the year, but we both agreed we just couldn't do anything against the law. I was so thankful I had purchased a beef cow, for now was the time to butcher both of them and concentrate on building the dairy herd. I can NOW see how God was in control of my life at an early age. My dairy soon became a herd of five: two cows, two heifers, and one bull.

Before going off to college I to be home to milk the cows by 7:00 p.m. EVERY evening (most the time I'd milk them at five). So I decided to move into the hayloft to sleep. I would get up at 4:00 a.m., jog to the house, grab the milking machine and extra large milk can, put them in the wheelbarrow and run them back to the barn in order to start milking at 4:30 a.m. This gave me enough time to measure, screen the milk, clean the machine, eat breakfast and head off the half mile walk to catch the school bus.

This routine would go on nearly all year and getting up at 4 a.m. made it easy to fall asleep at 7:30 p.m. Fact is, during graduation my friend had to use her elbow to awaken me a couple of times. I did leave right after graduation and even beat my parents home, so I could go to sleep.

My mother NEVER complained about milking those cows while I went off to college. I had acquired a refrigerator, purchased a milk machine and vacuum pump, built a milking parlor and rebuilt a 16' x 48' barn. We left the door to the house unlocked so Fox Island folks could walk in, select the milk from the refrigerator at anytime of the day. They just put the money in the cup we kept in the refrigerator, wrote down what they purchased, and return the old glass milk jugs. That's how things were back on Fox Island during the 60's and 70's. I don't know anyone who locked their house back then.

DON'T EAT THE RAISINS
1970

Over and over again I learned the importance of obeying my parents. I would learn, mess up and then learn the lesson again. I can remember my mother telling us 10 children not to get into the raisins. She tried to point out the importance of savoring special, expensive treats. More raisins meant more oatmeal cookies, or something to put into our warm mush or oatmeal in the morning.

My most vivid memory of a time I disobeyed came at 3:00 a.m. when I was in the ninth grade. I suddenly opened my eyes and thought... raisins! Sneaking off the top bunk of the triple layered bed, I quietly made my way out of the bedroom. After peering around each corner and avoiding the squeaky step on the stairs, I entered the kitchen. Opening the cupboard, I could just make out the big bag of raisins in the dim light. I jammed my fist into the bag and grabbed one handful after another. They hit the spot as my hunger pain subsided. Stopping at two handfuls allowed me to escape my mother's notice.

Waking up before anyone else, I once again sneaked into the kitchen, this time in the morning light. The sun shone through the kitchen window and illuminated the large raisin bag. I slowly pulled the noisy sack from its place of rest. I once again jammed my hand in and pulled out a large handful. This time something looked different. With the light of day shining on my handful of raisins, I could see large white maggots squirming in and out of the slimy brown fruit. I quickly threw the fly larvae back into the sack and went right to Mom to report my act of disobedience.

The lesson I learned that day came from John 3:19. The light shone onto what I had eaten in darkness and after finding out the truth I never wanted to go back to disobeying my mother again. I wish I was successful in my desire to do what is right all the time. As a Christian I have learned that I can never be perfect, but I can continue to strive forward as being obedient to God.

FALLING OFF THE BARN ROOF
1971

Mike Ford may have been younger than me, but he was a good friend all the same. I remember when he came over and helped me mix and pour the concrete for my milking parlor. Fact is, his name and the date are still etched in the concrete floor.

He was one of those people who ALWAYS cared about others. He was trying to get me back in Boy Scouts, which now I WISH I had heeded his advice. He was also trying to get me to go back to church which, once again, I WISH I had listened to him. He was genuinely careful and wise not to push too hard for I was in the middle of my infamous teenage rebellion years. Oh how I wish I could go back in time and correct my foolish ways, how they haunt me. My greatest prayer is that my grandchildren will learn from the foolish mistakes of their grandpa and be wiser as they navigate their teenage years.

A note to my grandchildren: So many mistakes people have made been over the years/centuries. Learn from them so you won't have to agonize because you made the same ones. Be wise and listen to older people who love you.

Back to the story. So, one day Mike Ford was helping me put the roof on the barn. It was about 16' to the peak, 60 feet long and 16 feet wide. The pitch was about 6/12 which allowed enough room for a loft upstairs. The day before it had rained, so the plywood was VERY slick. We started with the saturated felt. As I started shimming across the ridge, I realized I had forgotten the staple gun. So I yelled to Mike, "Hey Mike, throw the staple gun my way." He was such a good help and I really appreciated it.

Did I mention that he was a sensitive, and caring person? Well, Mike didn't want the staple gun to hit me, so he slid it very gently in my direction. It came up 12" short, BUT I thought if I could stretch a little further I could get it. As I stretched out, I lost my grip on the ridge and started down the 16' plywood roof, gaining speed as I went. It was a real hopeless feeling (should have thought right then and there that it was the same feeling I had as a teen) down, down, faster and faster until I flipped off the edge and started towards the ground. Mike reminded me that I had yelled, "Dagnabit!" For even being a teen I refused to swear, which will be another story.

I headed straight down towards the ground, and in a split second I saw a pile of barn boards stacked and leaning nicely against one sawhorse. My heavy WWII combat boots hit the ends of the boards, at first breaking my fall, BUT, also causing the boards to fly into the air. They came back down and hit in unison causing me to fly back up into the air, flipping me once 360 degrees. Maybe it was my heavy boots, but now I was coming back to earth AGAIN feet first. I hit the soft ground like an acrobat, arms straight out, knees bent, and springing on my toes. Mike told me later that I said, "Tadaa!" as I landed on the ground.

I was not aware that my mother was watching the entire incident from the house. She later explained that it caused her heart to stop. Poor Mike was frozen in place, fearing that he had just killed me. It was all the persuasion I could figure in my little teenage brain to convince Mike that it wasn't his fault. To this day he still blames himself, but we both laugh at how it ended. Needless to say I decided to wait until the plywood was dry before attempting that again

GROWING UP ONE DAY
1971

In 1964 my parents purchased land that went from the kelp line back a quarter of a mile for $1,500. They then had our five bedroom house built up on the bluff for $15,000. The view on our left included the Tacoma Narrows Bridge, straight across was Tacoma and Mount Rainer, slightly to the right we could see Mount Saint Helens, and Mount Adams, and on our far right we saw Anderson Island, Steilacoom and the Nisqually Flats. No one wanted property so far away. My neighbor, Farmer Browne told me about land that went for 25 cents per acre before the ferry and bridges (Narrows and Fox Island). It was just very hard to get to and from the island. Mr. Browne purchased land along Island Boulevard, just south of the big tree and land over by Etlow (Pebble Beach), a farm with a large barn that is located across from what is now the yacht club, the big farm on 14th Ave, and other places.

Then the land prices started to increase which meant taxes soon followed. I had no idea of how economics worked, the amount of taxes for land, or the relationship between them. I was a child and only knew that I LOVED living on Fox Island and thought life would never change. I knew we were not rich, but didn't know how poor we really were until one morning.

I had gone up the stairs to eat breakfast and noticed my dad was sitting there
with his elbows on the table holding the sides of his head. Just the look on his face told of a turmoil stirring inside. Pop and I never talked deep or opened up to each other. Mom on the other hand, well, we were like pals when it came to philosophy and the way of the world. We would talk, discuss issues and it only drew us closer. This one morning my dad looked all bummed out, even depressed looking. So I asked him, "Pop, what's

wrong?"

At first he was very hesitant, but then he spilled his guts. "I have two weeks to pay the taxes or lose this place. We will have to move, but there is nowhere to go." If ANY high school boy ever heard such a statement from his father he would be instantly changed for life. I was in shock, and it was all I could think about for the entire day. I went to school, did my school work, came home and worked…all the while thinking to myself, "How am I going to fix this?"

The next day I had decided to drop out of high school and go to work until my Grandma Kibler's boyfriend, Igan, confronted me. "Daniel," he said, "you MUST finish high school! Don't EVER think about dropping out."

Deep down I knew he was right, so I hung in there and worked after school. I had several jobs, construction with Paul Wise, working on Browne's farm, and expanding my dairy. No more sports or vacation, no senior pictures, no dances, no ASB card, no more childhood, because I had to do or move… I read many survival books and learned how to forage for food. Besides the massive about of food from the beach, I learned how to eat stinging nettles and make a lovely tea. I became VERY focused on surviving the taxman and providing food for the family. One time my dad and I were so tempted to get fish that we discussed taking the long fishing net at night and stringing it out then pulling it back in early in the morning. I was shocked that I was the one that said, "I really don't want to get caught doing anything illegal." My dad quickly agreed while shaking his head as if to say, "I can't believe I thought of something so wrong!"

Dogfish was a staple for us. They were easy to catch and one fish with potatoes could feed the entire family…well, feed the ones that were left anyway, eight of us. At one point the old Fox Island store turned into a herring packing plant. Mrs. Walker would give us a call whenever a dogfish came in (mixed with the herring). I remember driving to the "store" and seeing all the ladies along an assembly line putting the herring on square paper plates then wrapping plastic around each plate. I am not sure how they knew we needed food, (maybe they didn't) but just knew we wanted the dogfish. When cleaning these small sharks we would slam the head onto a board that had a nail sticking out. With the nail holding its head we'd simply make two cuts around the gills and pull the skin right off. We'd place the meat in a bowl of lemon juice to neutralize the uric acid.

The next day they were ready to cook.

For over four years, I was obsessed with making sure we had enough food for the family and money for taxes. One September Pop went back to college (WSU) on the WWII GI bill so we only saw him when the school was out on vacation. Mom took over the finances and I continued working every job and every minute I had. I was going full throttle totally 100% hardworking. At the time, I only knew one other high school student that was as hard working as I was. He quickly became my friend and we'd talk about how much fun it was working from sun up to sun down. It's interesting to me how quickly teens can find others who have the same interest. His name is Dwayne and to this day we are friends, although not as close due to distance.

I left in 1979 to marry my wonderful bride and start our own family. My dad had also graduated from WSU, got a teaching job and was able to hold back the taxman for a couple more years. In 1982, after both my mother and father retired they became overwhelmed with the taxes and gave in. They sold their dream home and moved into a single wide mobile home in Moclips, Washington, where in 2002 Pop took his last breath.

Mom then moved in with Mary and is very happy just living with the many good memories of living on Fox Island.

Nearly every teenager I know would have done the same thing. Flash back to December 7, 1941, and see how the youth responded to the attack on our country. It makes me wonder if it's really all that bad when our youth must grow up before they're 20? The youth of America freed the world, THEN turned each country BACK to the people, so they could control their own lives. Years later, when I was the vice principal I decided to perform an experiment. I came upon a table of students that, well, you might say was a troubled lot. They thought of themselves as gangsters. I posed a scenario: "Tell me, what if we had an earthquake and as you were walking home, you could hear kindergarten children trapped in the rubble. Would you help them? If yes then how long before you got tired of moving the bricks?"

The leader looked up at me and said, "Mr. Bushnell, we would NEVER get tired we would NEVER stop until EVERY child was out." Yep, that confirmed it in my mind.

As an adult I found that many children, like myself, find different ways to rebel. Some will dye their hair blue, while others will pierce their forehead. I grew my hair long. My mother always said, "It's usually just a way for a child to scream out for attention. Give it to them." I loved supervising during lunch time, since that gave me time to sit at the tables of many different students. Especially ones who needed attention and validity from adults.

One day my mother told me how to treat teenagers. She said once you've made it through the rough teen valley you must act like an adult. The teens will see you and find many ways to cry out to you. You must stay firm on the outer edge, standing on the rock of truth. Call out to each one, giving guidance for them to make it through. But you MUST stand firm, and don't go back into the teenage valley, but keep shining your light for them. Catch their attention with the fishhook of love and even though they will fight you and swim from one side to the other they will eventually make it out. And when they do, you'll have a friend for life.

TAKING CONTROL
1971

The one issue with digging fencepost holes was the clay. Eight inches below the top soil was the infamous clay. To this day I'll swear it is the most pure clay I have ever seen...even the blocks you purchase at a craft store aren't as pure. The issue is that it's very difficult to pack around the post, so I had to put a bucket of beach gravel around each post in order to pack the "dirt." Every year another dairy cow would calf and I needed more grazing pasture. Grandma Kibler let me use her land, but I'd have to fence it in first. So there I would go down the steep grade to the beach, fill two buckets of gravel and grunt my way back up the steep hill and out towards the end of the pasture. The fence along 14th Ave. was a quarter mile from the beach. It was hard work, but you did what had to be done and I didn't have a tractor to haul the gravel, so away I went bucket after bucket of rocks and shells. This had to be done so I could sell and provide milk. The money from the milk would allow me to graduate from college and the milk I didn't sell provided much needed nourishment for our family. As a teen I loved the autonomy my parents gave me and everything about the island on which I lived.

One day Joe saw me working away hauling buckets of gravel to the field and came up with a "better" idea. "Let's use the wheelbarrow and hitch up the three little boys." So we filled the barrow to the top and hitched Tom, Larry, and Ed with ropes to the wheelbarrow. I struggled to lift the barrow and away we went. It looked like a slug racing competition. The three boys were grunting as their feet would dig in and give way up the incline. I would struggle keeping the wheelbarrow level as I pushed. Joe was the master of ideas as he yelled encouragement...well, not sure if yelling, "mush, mush..." was encouragement, but that's what he called it.

Today was one of those very rare days when the temperature topped 90 degrees and we had just crested the top of the very steep hill. The wheelbarrow was full of gravel, the three "little" boys hitched up working like borrowed mules, and me still struggling to keep it level. We rounded the corner and headed towards the barn when in an instant my life changed. All I could see were tiger paws, just before everything went black! Crash, the wheelbarrow went over, I went down, and the world went dark. Thankfully Joe was an EMT and knew exactly what had happened, heat stroke. To this day I have a very hard time working in direct sun or when it's over 75 degrees out.

I was carried to the house, rehydrated and told to lie there until my temperature went back to normal. I had a very difficult time laying there doing NOTHING. Moms have a way of making you do things you don't want to do, so the rest of the day I laid on the couch and "rested." It was seriously one of the most difficult things to do knowing someone was outside working, doing your work, while you were inside laying on the couch!

This was an awakening for others, but it wasn't until after retirement I noticed anything wrong with me. I was proud to be a hardworking man, putting in more hours than anyone else and more than what was required. When asked what I would like for my birthday, I would say tools or supplies (wheelbarrow, saws, fencing). I remember getting my own wheelbarrow for my 16th birthday. My dad and a couple of my teachers saw the road I was on and tried to warn me… "Daniel," they would say, "You need to play, and need to relax some and enjoy life."

I replied, "You don't understand, working is play! Every time I build something, or when I dig a ditch for power to the barn, it feels good. It's better than doing something that accomplishes NOTHING!"
My dad purchased an AM FM radio for my 15th birthday and said, "You need to enjoy life more. So relax and listen to music or something." I thought my dad was very strange…but now I can see that he was right.

The problem with being a workaholic is that it's worn as a badge of honor. It's like how driving while drunk used to be viewed as humorous. Now that I am in my 60's, I have come to realize that IT'S NOT FUNNY or a badge of honor! My own children suffered from me working so much. Here's an example: in my job as a vice principal I supervised MANY after school activities, usually sporting events. I would arrive at 4:30 every morning (sometimes earlier) and come home after an athletic event. Twenty three years of freely putting in all those hours, I retired. Now I go back to the school to enjoy an evening event and it cost me $6.00. Yes, that's right, I donated 23 years of my life, two to three times a week to keep the gym/field safe and that's it… "who are you again"…asks the new fool? If it wasn't for my fabulous bride, my daughters would have turned out much differently without Dad being around.

My eyes started opening when I saw my son-in-law working hard, BUT the difference is that he enjoy vacations, he's relaxed and not everything has to be done now. One day he mentioned to me that he was so excited about this summer. "I get to go skeet shooting with my church friends in June, I am going fishing out of Westport in July, going to Silverwood in Idaho with the family in August, and to cap it all off I'll be going to a men's retreat at Malibu Camp in Canada in September!"

I was thinking I was going to enjoy the summer too, I would build a new woodshed, a bunkhouse at Ocean Shores, put in two year's firewood, and pick berries for the winter." I was going to the same places with him (Silverwood, Fishing, Men's Retreat...), however, I thought of those activities and as things to check off a list so I could get back to accomplishing something. Dustin was living and looking forward to doing things with others. Being a workaholic is NOT funny.

Sure workaholism can still sneak up on you, but I have found that the Lord has given me a second chance in life, grandchildren. I heard a song that described my life, it's called; "Cat's in The Cradle" and I ache EVERYTIME I hear it. But not anymore! I refuse to chase the almighty dollar, or get my fulfillment/satisfaction by working to the extreme. Now I don't set a strict time limit to fill an order for lumber and I tell my customers that if my grandchildren want to play catch your order may be done later. When my grandchildren ask me to throw the football with them, well, I throw the football with them. We build forts, play games, watch a show, go to the movies, build things together, play, and hang out. I still get things done, but it doesn't control my life.

A VISIT FROM THE HUMANE SOCIETY
1972

I decided to give my brother Tom a chance to tell one of the many adventures we had while growing up on Fox Island.

I grew up on "the far end of Fox Island" in the southern Puget Sound in the 60's and 70's. We had a five bedroom house for our family of two parents (both of which were a bit hard of hearing), eight boys and two girls. We were a poor family, but we never went hungry because between the dog fish the commercial salmon fishermen would throw on shore for us and our goats, rabbits, and chickens we did alright. Later my brother raised some beef cows, but that is another story for another day. The front door to our house was a sliding glass door that opened into our dining room.

One day in about 1972, I was walking up from the barn toward the house. In our parking area, I saw one of those new fangled "economy cars." It looked like a little white tin box, and on the door in blue paint were the words, "Tacoma Pierce County Human Society." I had no idea what that meant, but it looked official.

As I came through the sliding glass front door, I saw Mom, with her back to the door and the Humane Society lady across the table with some papers spread out in front of her. The Humane Society lady had a good view of everyone coming in the door. We did not get very many guests, living out in the boondocks and all; so my mom was pretty excited to have another lady to talk with… and talk they did. From the gist of the conversation I picked up that there was some new law that required dogs to have licenses. I had a hard time getting my head around that. Why would a dog need a license? After all they don't drive, at least I had never heard of a dog that drove. The cost for the license for our two dogs was going to be $4.00 each, a total of $8.00. To a ten year old that seemed like a heap sum of money.

Well, Mom and that lady must have really hit it off. They talked for over an hour. In the meantime, my brother, Dan, went down to the barn to butcher a rabbit for dinner. Mom made a mean rabbit stew. I can still taste it. Dan finished butchering the rabbit. Did I mention that we had rabbit butchering races? Dan was the undisputed rabbit butchering champion; he could kill, skin and clean a rabbit in just under two minutes.

On the way to the house with the skinned and cleaned rabbit, Dan saw the stranger's car in the parking area. He walked in the door and held up the skinned rabbit so the Humane Society lady could get a good view of it. Dan just held it up there a moment for effect and said, "Hey Mom, I finally caught the neighbor's cat!"

Mom was busy talking away and didn't pay much attention to what Dan said. Mom merely replied, "Great! Throw it in the sink and we'll have it for dinner!"

I was watching this all transpire from just around the corner. The Humane Society lady turned pale white, folded up her paperwork, ran out to her car and drove away without so much as one word. Mom was flummoxed and simply said, "Now why do you suppose she acted so rudely?" We had to explain to Mom what had actually transpired. She was pretty upset at first, but with everyone laughing so hard all around her she could not stay upset for long.

We were never forced to get licenses for our dogs, as the Humane Society lady never came by our home again. However and we had some tasty rabbit stew that night.

HILLBILLIES AT A PROPER WEDDING; WHAT COULD GO WRONG?
1972

This was the first wedding all seven of us boys ever attended. We'd attended football games, we'd ridden cows, we'd taken our goat camping, we'd played cow pie baseball, and even walked a goat on the Narrows Bridge...BUT we had never traveled all the way across the state to attend a wedding. Some of us felt pretty proud knowing some wedding traditions, but most of us learned a lot that day. We learned that they cut cake (even though one of our brothers told us that in Wisconsin they cut a big block of cheese, not cake), decorated a car, and walked down an aisle. We learned that the bride wore a special dress, exchanged rings...all kinds of neat things. Have you ever heard the song, "Who let the dogs out?" Well, for us it was like letting the clowns out... "Who let the clowns out?"

Joe kind of started the entertainment while sitting in the truck and yelling to Pop that there was something wrong with it. When Pop came over and peered under the hood, Joe honked the horn. Pop's head jerked up and it hit the hood really hard. He wasn't too happy about that.

Then we had some "on the job training" when it came to decorating the wedding car. Tom, Larry, and Ed learned from Pop that you DO NOT spray shaving cream ALL over the inside of the car. I learned that shaving cream takes the paint off the outside of a car. Joe and John learned that you don't switch all the spark plug wires around so the car won't start. Thank goodness Pop stopped us before the tires were hidden. He cleaned the entire car before anything was damaged. Tim came out and re-organized the leads on the car so it would start before Ilene came out and killed all of us (as you can tell, we deserved it).

Here's how I remember the next part of the wedding. Well, if the truth be known, Tom wasn't actually trying to catch the bouquet. At the time he had no clue what was going on (he had NEVER been to a wedding and Mom kept him on the island and wouldn't let him out much). All he knew was that he was just walking along (while Ilene and all the ladies were setting up for the bouquet toss) and he looked up and saw a bouquet of flowers flying through the air. He had NEVER seen a bouquet of flowers flying before, so he did what any cat would do. He jumped to knock it out of the air. Everyone thought he was trying to catch it. At the time I was filming the event and caught some of it on tape. He got in a lot of trouble by the ladies and Pop, but he looked like a deer caught in the headlights...since he had no clue he did anything wrong. I can't remember, but I think some of the ladies were knocked to the ground when he jumped. It was a funny event for us boys, since we too had no clue why Ilene decided to throw the bouquet.

Tom did say his older brother, John, whispered in his ear to go catch that bouquet, BUT after catching it a very tall girl ripped it from his grasp and gave him the stink eye. I think it was Ilene's best lady (see I now know everything about weddings).

The one thing Ilene's side of the family enjoyed was that they didn't have to pay for any entertainment. Who let the clowns out? Woof woof!

John sneaks out from behind a tree and tells what REALLY happened

Tom was in about 6th grade when Tim and Ilene got married. He was a very big and aggressive boy for his age. Tom also liked competition, especially when he won. So right before Ilene was to throw the bouquet to all the unmarried ladies, I whispered to him, 'They're about ready for the traditional contest to see who is the best at catching the bouquet of flowers; it's just like playing football.' Then I told him he should go down and see if he's good enough to catch it. Ilene was ready to throw it while I was still speaking to Tom.

We were standing well above and off to the side of where the ladies had gathered. In order for Tom to make it in time, he would need to run down about 25 feet, then around a concrete wall that had a black rod iron fence on it and then he would need to go another 30 feet just to get within striking distance of where the pack of ladies had gathered. Within a split second after I told Tom he should see if he could catch the bouquet, he was flying down to the end of the concrete wall, grabbing the rod iron fence with his left hand which helped him fling his body into position so that he would be running with a full head of steam by the time he intersected with the gathered pack that stood between him and winning. Ilene was waving the bouquet and savoring the moment as she surveyed her band of friends who had gathered with hopes of being the next one chosen for marital bliss. As she released the flowers they arched up into the air, over her friends, hands and arms stretched upward like a wave on a foaming sea. Just as the flowers' arch started to descend Tom was at maximum speed, his eyes focused upon the prize. Leaping like a mighty killer whale with arms fully stretched out, he impaled the wave causing bodies to fling in every direction like bowling pins in a strike zone. As he plowed through the wave of bodies, his hands clenched the prize bouquet. Then as quickly as he blew the place apart, his feet gracefully hit the ground while thrusting the bouquet upward standing tall like the Statue of Liberty, he proclaimed with a loud voice, "I got it, I WIN!"

As I watched this unfold, I was so beside myself that I thought I was having an out of body experience. I crumpled to the ground as tears of laughter streamed down my face. Unfortunately, laying on the ground in uncontrollable laughter, I was unable to see what fallout was happening below.

WHAT NOT TO SAY
1972

I was SO clumsy around girls
that it was either totally embarrassing
or hilariously funny…in other words,
I was clueless. In tenth grade, there
was this one girl that just moved in
from the big city named Janeen. She was quite wise to the world, since she
lived around people all her life.

After a couple of weeks of riding the school bus, I got the courage to
sit with her…IN THE SAME SEAT!!! It was a pretty big deal. After a week
or two of just sitting there, I decided to say, "Hi." Things really progressed
from there. I would say, "Hi! How are you doing?" Yes, I practiced for
several days each morning as I went out to milk the cows. I didn't even
need note cards or anything. I just blurted out, "Hi, how are you doing?"

Well, after a couple of months, I really got a liking to this city girl. She
was so knowledgeable about things like…well, after 6th grade I had no clue
about when Valentine's Day was or what you're supposed to do about
it…she knew those type of things. Please remember there were eight boys
in our family and Valentine's Day… let's just say it didn't cross my radar.

Okay, here is where I lost my Janeen FOREVER! I was going to tell
her that I liked her. So, once again I practiced and practiced, yes, while
feeding the cows. I didn't say it the first couple of days as I was just too
chicken, BUT I finally got the courage to say something…AND I said it
ALL WRONG, but didn't know it for YEARS. I got on the empty bus and
silently watched as it progressed from one stop to the next, slowly filling as
the children boarded. I became more and more nervous at every passing
minute, but there was nothing I could do as the bus got closer and closer to
her stop. Finally Janeen got on, and slowly walked down the aisle until she
got to my seat (okay it was the ONLY seat left since she was the LAST stop
and everyone left it for her OR it might have been no one would sit with
me, not sure.) She swung around and gracefully glided down as in slow
motion. That is when I said it, "Janeen, I like you!" I think it would have
been okay if I just didn't open my mouth and try to explain how
much…but I continued. "Janeen, I like you so much…I am going to name
every cow I have after YOU!!" Her eyes went real big. She looked at me as

though she was looking at Sasquatch. At first I thought she was impressed, but her disposition told me otherwise. I knew that very day I had said SOMETHING wrong, but couldn't figure out what it was.

It was the last day she rode the bus, and I don't know if I ever saw her again. BUT, a promise is a promise...to keep your promise is VERY important. So I gave every one of my cattle, dairy and beef Janeen's name. I wish she had said it was okay not to and now I know why...so the best way to keep my word was to give all of them the name Janeen as a middle name. Annabelle Janeen Cow, Arabelle Janeen Cow, Wheelabarrow Janeen Cow, Grannybelle Janeen Cow, Larrabelle Janeen Cow...and it continued. There are more names, but ALL with Janeen as their middle name. Glad tattoos weren't common back then!

Years later, I met my bride and she explained to me that girls do NOT like being compared to cows. My bride is so patient and good to me!!! She is also from the city and told me, much later that she had NEVER met anyone like me. At first she was just curious to see if I was for real or just kidding around. Well, it didn't take long for her, to realize someone was going to have to teach me about the world and she fell in love with me trying. Do you know what the Lord has done? Gave me FOUR daughters! For the past 40 YEARS I have been out numbered...tell you one thing though, I will NEVER name a cow after a girl again!!

TERRORIZED BY A CHICKEN
1972

I think I mentioned before, "The biggest gifts we received were found on the beach at the high tide mark." After a storm one winter day, I found a four to five foot Styrofoam board. I thought it was a surfboard, but later discovered it was called a "boogie board." On this particular day, I didn't care what it was called as I was just upset.

It was 4:30 am as I headed to the barn for the morning milking, when, to my dismay, I discovered my boogie board, broken into small chunks. The dastardly perpetrator didn't even hide the evidence. I became very upset and made a beeline straight back to the house. I grabbed Ed awake and yelled, "What did you do to my surfboard!"

Not letting him answer I continued, "Why did you break it up into small chunks?"

I knew in the back of my mind that none of this made sense. We didn't have much money so no one really went around to intentionally destroy something. It would have been as much a treasure for Ed as it was for me.

"I didn't break it, I didn't break it!" Ed kept repeating, "That chicken you brought home broke it into bits." I couldn't believe what I was hearing. Ed was attempting to blame a chicken on breaking up my Styrofoam surfboard? He continued, "That chicken you brought home is a killer!!! It came after me with its beak, claws, and wings. I grabbed the surfboard so it wouldn't kill me and it tore it to bits, ripping it out of my hands. I ran away as fast as I could. I am so sorry it destroyed your board!" As he told this tale, his voice kept raising louder and louder, as it took on a shaking sound, while his eyes got wider and wider. "I am afraid to go down to feed the chickens because of that killer! It comes after me, even in my dreams, and sometimes it won't let me out of the chicken coop."

I still couldn't believe what I was hearing. Just a couple days ago our bus driver, Howard, had a friend who had to get rid of his chickens and asked me if I wanted a rooster. Well, he didn't have to ask me twice. After all, who wouldn't want a free chicken. He brought it over and I let it run with the others. It looked to be larger than our Plymouth Rock and Road Island Reds that Ed and Larry took care of so I figured there had to be more meat on that big bird. What Howard's friend failed to tell him, or me, is that it was a trained fighter and used to keep the neighbor's pit bull out of his yard. I had never heard of such a thing and refused to believe Ed when he adamantly exclaimed that it was a killer. How could this be true, since I had never heard of it before? I was 14 years old. At the time, I thought I knew just about everything there was to know.

I was still upset about the surfboard and refused to believe Ed. So, ignoring the facts I forced Ed out of bed and compelled him to go down to the barn with me. He started resisting and pleading, "PLEASE DAN, hit me, punch me, I don't care, just don't make me go down there again!! I am having nightmares because of that killer chicken!"

After his request I started to think, "What is it about Ed and that chicken? Maybe he's telling me the truth, OR maybe I don't hit hard enough?"

I had Ed by the scruff of the neck and was marching him down to the chicken coop when we spotted the rooster. At the same time it spotted us. Evidently that large white leghorn chicken hadn't lasted long in the pen and was out roaming the barnyard. The chicken was only 30 feet away when Ed started to flail to the point where I couldn't hold him any longer. He bolted straight for the chicken house and closed himself in while the leghorn eyed me. I had a flash of what it must have felt like during the shoot-out at the Okay Corral. It puffed its feathers and wings out a bit and took two steps towards me. I hesitantly took two steps towards the rooster, but in the back of my mind I was attempting to make sense of this surreal experience. The rooster ducked its head down a little, then stretched its neck out, pointing his beak right at me. I stopped. He didn't. It took deliberate steps, one at a time straight towards me. I just froze while my young brain tried desperately to synthesize all this new information. 'A killer chicken? How can this be? It's a chicken. Seriously, I am not chicken of this chicken, am I?' It kept getting closer and closer until within 15 feet it seemed like it was shot out of a cannon, as it let out a loud scream and propelled itself straight towards my face.

I took off running towards the chicken house, flung open the door, grabbed it again and slammed it just in time. The chicken hit the outside of the door, latched onto the board and batten siding and attempted to peck a hole through it trying to get to us. Now it was my turn to be scared to death. The bird continued pecking as I yelled over the noise, "ED WHAT DO WE DO NOW?"

He simply said, "Follow me." As he got on his knees and crawled out the small 12" chicken hole, down the short ramp, into the chicken pen, ran to the barn where the pen was attached, opened the parlor door, worked his way 50 feet through the barn to the opposite end and ran to the house. While milking the cows that morning, I caught myself looking over my shoulder several times.

It was difficult concentrating at school that day while thinking about the near-death experience with that killer chicken. I didn't want to tell my friends since I knew they would just laugh, as I did, when Ed explained the situation. I did however, devise a plan to capture that chicken for dinner.

We had a half mile walk after the long bus ride home, so I had more time to iron out a plan. Before I could implement it, I opened the sliding glass door to find Igan sitting there with a stern look on his face. I didn't know what I did wrong, but just knew it was bad when my grandma's boyfriend told me to, "Sit down and listen." Here's what he told me:

"Dan, you MUST kill that chicken and do it TODAY!" I tried to explain that I was going to do that very thing when he stopped me, "Stop, listen!" He continued, "I want you to know what happened today. I was enjoying the sunshiny day while sitting in the shade of the moon garden. Your grandma was weeding the garden and as you know she is very short and has bad knees. When she weeds she simply bends over locking her knees in place and goes at it. She can stay in that position for hours pulling weeds like a Tasmanian Devil; she is a very unique woman. While rocking back and forth, I noticed some movement up by your barn. It took me a while for my eyes to focus, but I saw your chicken about 200 feet away walking straight towards your grandmother. That chicken didn't deviate to the left or right, but made a bee line up over the compost bin, jumped over the bushes, like a laser beam straight towards your grandma. Did I mention to you how grandma weeds? Can you imagine how exposed her bottom was sticking up in the air like that?

"I didn't realize you had a killer chicken! You should NEVER have accepted that type of chicken," he shouted.

I started thinking to myself, "Does EVERYONE know about killer chickens and forgot to tell me? I don't think they taught us in school about killer chickens."

Igan continued, "Before I could react, it was too late. That killer chicken burst forward at a speed I had never seen before and attached itself to your grandma's backside. She let out with a loud scream and took off across the yard, turned and came back past me. All the while that bird was chasing her with its wings out and head down. I had NEVER seen your grandma run so fast and long. Around and around the yard they went until somehow she got into the house. She is in there right now and refuses to come out. She won't even let me in until that chicken is killed."

I let Igan know that he could count on me. "I'll get rid of that killer from our farm," I confirmed.

I immediately gathered three machetes, then went back upstairs and waited and waited until the three little boys came home from elementary school. Perhaps it wasn't very wise of me to give a machete to second, third, and fourth grade students, but I did. I lined them up, looked straight into their eyes, walking back and forth in front of them, like a drill sergeant, and said in a serious voice, "Do you think you're old enough to go on a mission?

"YES, WE ARE!" they yelled in unison.

"Okay then, IF you think you're brave enough then here's the mission; take your machete and go kill a chicken!"

It was about here that Ed said, "WHAT? What chicken do you want us to kill?"

It's okay Ed, you can do this," and I patted him on the shoulder and moved the three boys out the door.

I could hear Tom's sing-song voice, "We're going to kill a chicken, were going to kill a chicken!" As they headed down to the barn. Ed was about 20 feet behind the other two, but to my dismay continued in the same direction. I went to the laundry room to watch from the second story window.

I could still hear Tom singing his, "going to kill a chicken song." I held my breath as Tom got closer and closer to that killer chicken. He didn't even notice the warning signs that big creature created. Its head bobbed down, and Ed stopped, but Tom and Larry kept moving closer. The killer took two steps closer, and Tom and Larry didn't stop. Then it happened, the killer chicken charged Tom at full force, flipped its talons straight at Tom's chest and latched on. It then proceeded to attempt to peck a hole in

Tom's chest.

One thing I forgot to tell you about Tom. Tom feels no pain, well, at least he never seems to anyway. He's the one who could put his hand on the electric fence the longest. We always had Tom check and see if the fence was on before we crossed over. He was just downright tough, even before he started first grade. Everyone in our family would agree; he was the toughest of the 10 children and when in high school became a first-string defensive lineman for the state champion football team. We all thought he'd keep going to college football, but he chose not to because he did not think it was worth the risk of having his knees blown out.

As the chicken pecked and pecked at Tom's chest he started yelling, "I caught it, I caught it!" And was swinging his machete in front of his face trying to bring it down on the chicken as it was latched onto his chest.

I heard Larry yell, "I'll get it Tom" as he started swinging his machete at the chicken that was near Tom's head. My heart stopped, and I stopped breathing as I watched my two younger brothers swinging machetes right past Tom's face. Once or twice their machetes collided and a loud "clang" sound resonated. Finally, Larry hit the chicken which caused it to tumble to the ground.

Tom picked it up by its feet, turned towards the house, and started chanting, "We killed the chicken, we killed the chicken!" I could see Tom's shirt covered in his own blood. He just didn't care, he was so excited about killing the chicken.

I gladly gathered the machetes and thought to myself, "I will NEVER do that again!" Then I told the boys how proud I was of them completing the mission and that they could now go downstairs and watch Gilligan's Island.

Mary started dinner before Mom got home, but we left the chicken for Mom. She was the fastest person in the world at plucking the feathers off a bird since she grew up with chickens during the Great Depression. Mom was so proud of me when I told her that I had killed a chicken for dinner and had the scalding water ready for the dipping. It's easier to get the feathers off a bird when you dip them in a pot of scalding water, What I didn't know is that Larry hadn't really killed the chicken, but had knocked it out.

I felt a bit too prideful as I watched Mom grab the feet of that killer and dip it in the hot water. That's when we discovered the killer chicken wasn't dead, but just knocked out. It came back out of that hot water and attacked Mom. She went running around the big dining room table screaming for me to, "Kill it kill it." Evidently, she too knew about killer chickens. Tom and Larry came running up the stairs and started chasing the chicken that was chasing Mom. At some point we were able to get our hands on it and finally kill the bird.

I felt bad taking credit for killing that killer chicken and Mom found some words of wisdom to teach me about pride and taking credit that belonged to others. She is one of the wisest people I have ever known. No, I didn't have to eat crow, but we did have a great chicken soup!

WASHED UP ON THE BEACH
1972

Fence posts made from old growth cedar was the norm…some rich people purchased metal T-posts, but the salty air would do them in. After a storm, I would walk the beach to find new treasures and see how the landscape changed. Many new logs would appear, the banks would be a bit different, and trees would fall exposing new roots to be played on like monkey bars.

We had one particular storm that lasted a couple days and even when I took my "after storm walk" the wind was brisk. The tide was heading out, so I had a good 10' of beach to walk as I headed south towards the Old Concrete Dock. I approached a huge four foot in diameter log, I could hear the waters lapping at its side then spilling around the ends only to pull and roll the small rocks towards the next wave which would toss them up again. At first I couldn't tell if it was cedar until a very small chunk of bark appeared by a minute obscure bump. Fact is, it was the only bump on the entire thirty four foot solid cedar log.

The next day, with rope in hand I splashed my way down the beach at high tide towards the big log. During the cold winter months, I never bothered wearing cut-offs or taking my shoes and socks off since they were the only protection I had against the cold water. It took me several hours to maneuver that humongous log 1/2 mile along the beach, working it around a few rocks that protruded up. By the time I reached our beach, the tide was out at least 15 feet so I attached a cable from the floating log to the bank, and waited for the next day's high tide where I would inch it closer to the cliff.

At age 13, I started using the large family chainsaw that had a 36" bar. I think it was a Sears and Roebuck brand, but not sure. Saws back then didn't have self oilers so every few seconds you'd need to pump the oil button with your right thumb. I needed fence posts for the new pasture, so I started cutting the log one cant at a time, 7.5' feet long. I had to have that cant split and off the beach before the tide came back, otherwise they'd wash away. I went to work splitting off about 10 fence posts at a time then hauling them two at a time, one on each shoulder, up the steep,

steep road/trail to the second pasture past the barn. After five loads I'd split 10 more and start up the steep hill with fence posts on my shoulders. I was able to get around 45 or more posts per cant. It was hard work.

I think my mother got worried about me because three days later a friend, Carl, appeared at the top of the cliff. Carl was a year behind me in school and I think he kind of looked up to me a bit more than he should. He was also a VERY GOOD artist and could draw or paint nearly anything. I had JUST finished cutting the last cant and about a small four foot chunk remained. I didn't know what I was going to do with that last chunk, but I knew I had to get this cant off the beach. "Daniel!" Carl yelled and again, "Daniel!" Not sure how many times he called my name before I looked straight up and saw him.

"Hi Carl" I yelled back, "Do you want to split this log and make fence posts?" I could tell by his face that I had said something detestable and his response confirmed it. I ran up the steep driveway all the way to the front of our house (top of the cliff) where Carl was standing and gave him a manly hug. "What's up my friend?" I asked.

"We are going to Mount Rainier to do some sledding, want to come along?"

I declined and said, "Oh, that sounds like fun (I was only patronizing him), but I have this log I need to finish splitting into fence posts."

He became very assertive and scolded me, "YOU NEVER HAVE TIME TO DO ANYTHING FUN; YOU'RE ALWAYS WORKING!!!!" I was shocked to hear him say such a thing. Sure it was true, but what's wrong with that?

I quickly re-evaluated the situation...the last cant WAS tied to the bluff. The last four feet wasn't, but it just might be there when I get back...I hoped. But then, what was I going to do with that last piece anyway...maybe split it into tomato stakes? "Okay, I'll go."

Believe it or not I didn't even think about that log the entire day while sledding on Mount Rainier. The next morning I jumped out of bed and headed down to the log. The last cant was still in place, but as I feared, the last four foot piece was gone.

I started splitting it into fence posts when all of a sudden the cavalry appeared, yes, including a horse. My brother, Joe, became fascinated by this treasure I found. He ordered the three little boys (Tom, Larry, Ed and

YES the horse) to the beach to help split and carry the last of the posts back up. Joe quickly barked out orders as he organized a system to expedite the process. One time Joe set the wedge on the end for me to smack with the splitting maul; we all were in shock at how easy it was to split this old growth cedar. The wedge shot the 7.5 feet through the log and flew out the end, hitting Tom in the ankle. He let out with a howl and we all started laughing at his pain and our discovery. It was incredible how straight the grain was.

I continued making fence posts while Joe hitched up the horse. The boys would hook up four or five posts and away they'd go up the steep grade to the field behind the barn.

There were A LOT of trips pulling all 150 fence posts. I re-split a couple larger fence posts in order to make bean poles. I also traded 75 fence posts to Mr. Browne for a Sears and Roebuck Bradley Chainsaw...still have that saw. It was great being 15 years old and having my own chainsaw. I used the other posts to fence in the rest of the pasture for my beef and dairy cows. Some of those post are still sticking out of the ground after 50 years.

COWPIE BASEBALL
1973

Growing up on a secluded island, with nine siblings, and the freedom of not worrying about "what the neighbors might think" lent itself to our creative imaginations. This is a story about just one of those creative endeavors.

One of the many requirements for maintaining a good pasture is the breaking up of cow pies. If they were left alone the grass would grow thicker and luscious around them, but the cows wouldn't eat the grass. So, in order to keep the field from looking like chicken pox, we would put on our "clod hoppers" (WWII surplus combat boots). Then we would go out into the pasture and kick the cow pies apart. We boys had A LOT of laughs when finding a cow pie; we could kick far enough to hit a brother. Many times a brother would kick a cow pie really hard only to discover it was fresh. With a strong swift kick his boot would quickly pass through the manure, covering the boot with green goo. Many times a swift hard kick on a slippery, gooey pie would cause us to end up on our bottoms, on top of the pie. So if you find yourself in the cow pasture, kicking cow pies, be sure before you give it a hard kick that the pie has been sun baked.

I think it was Ed who came up with the brilliant idea of making this chore into a game of Cowpie Baseball. We set out the baseball diamond with a chunk of firewood to designate each base. Then everyone would scour the field, picking up all the cow pies we could find. Tom loved gathering horse biscuits from the neighbor's pasture which defeated one of our objectives, but added another dimension to Ed's game. We placed a large pile near each of the bases, but left the best cow pies for the pitcher, usually Ed. The best cow pies were ones that were sun baked on the outside, but still gooey in the middle. They were very rare, and when someone found one they'd let out with a loud hoot and howl, holding it straight out showing how solid it was, but then it would slowly started to sag. On one particular day we found one perfect cow pie, gooey in the center, but hard on the outside.

After there were enough pies, pieces of pies, and yes a few horse biscuits (thank you Tom) around the bases, Ed would go over the rules once again. "Okay everyone, you should already know how this works, but just in case you're new or you've forgotten I'll explain it once again." Many times we would invite fellow Fox Islanders for the fun and they might not know the rules. "As you can see there is a pile of pies near each base and the best ones are at the pitcher's mound. When the batter hits the ball, there are two ways you can get him out. One is with the ball and the other is by hitting him with a cow pie."

It was about this time Tom yelled, "OR HIT WITH A HORSE BISCUIT." He really had something about horse biscuits, Tom did.

Ed continued, "When a runner gets within 15 feet of a base, the man guarding that base is not allowed to throw a pie, piece of pie, or, yes Tom, a horse biscuit. You cannot chase the runner, but my advice is that when the runner gets close to your base you run away so you don't get hit by friendly fire. Are there any questions? Okay put in your potatoes to see who gets to go first."

We'd all gather around in a large circle with our fists touching as Ed sounded off. "One potato, two potato, three potato four, five potato, six potato, seven potato, more. Put that one behind your back." This would continue until the last man with a potato/fist would be the first up to bat. "Okay, Jim Edwards is up to bat. Take your positions."

Jim swung and missed the first pitch from Ed. Then Ed smeared a little brown "grease" on the ball, but Jim made contact so hard it went all the way to Mr. Brown's field and almost hit the big red barn. Then the storm started, a REAL manure storm. No one even looked at the ball or seemed to care that it had gone so far. Instead all you could see is a dark cloud of manure flying everywhere. Jim didn't hesitate, he took off like a deer caught in the orchard. As he rounded first base, Tom was trying his best to hit him with a horse biscuit (he called them hand grenades), but Jim was too quick with the side step. Then Ed picked up THE cow pie. You know, the one sun baked on the outside, but gooey in the middle. I guess it'd be best if I had Jim Edwards explain what he saw and heard:

"I had just rounded first base and headed for second. Everyone was missing me, as I dodged several pies and even Tom's horse biscuits, I was feeling pretty good. THEN, out of the corner of my left eye I saw Ed pick up that very special cow pie. The one that's gooey in the middle with a hard sun baked crust. All of a sudden I felt like I was in a dream where my feet wouldn't move fast enough. Everything just went into slow motion and even the sounds were all muffled as Ed slung it just like a Frisbee right towards me. I saw it rippling as it flew through the air and let off with a cadence like a heartbeat (thinking back the sound reminded me of that jaws movie). I kept trying to run harder and harder, but I couldn't get out of the way. Then I heard this loud splat as it hit my head and wrapped all the way around. It got into BOTH my ears, my eyes, my mouth and nose. I know it's gross, but looking back I never, in my entire life, had so much fun than visiting the Bushnell farm."

It wrapped all the way around Jim's head as he turned quickly, make his way to the cow's watering trough. We were laughing so hard no one could hear the noise he made when dunked, exhaling bubbles and shaking his head under water. It didn't take him long to clean off as Ed yelled out, "OKAY WHO'S NEXT?"

Tom quickly yelled, "ME, LET ME BE NEXT!"

Everyone has a story about getting hit with a cow pie or horse biscuit, but Jim Edwards was the only person ever to get hit in the head with a very special cow pie. Well, it was a lot more fun fertilizing the pasture while playing cow pie baseball than using our clod hoppers.

ISLANDERS HELP EACH OTHER
1973

I will NEVER forget how people ALWAYS helped each other on the island. When St. Aquinas School closed and Pop lost his day job as a teacher, nights and summers as a custodian, we quickly adjusted our thinking. There were no food banks back then...if there were a food banks no one would accept anything anyway (back then). People would always think that someone else had it worse. Welfare was "only for those in real need" so there was this sense of self-reliance and accepting help from neighbors and friends...NOT the government. Remember, the Great Depression was burned into the brains of the adults. IF there were food banks no one would withdraw food, but EVERYONE would donate to help others.

While working for Farmer Browne one cold, rainy, winter day, he asked why I didn't bring my coat. (I had been wearing Grandpa Ben's old WWI Navy coat, but it had finally given way to age). I explained what had happened to my coat and the next day I had a brand new Levi Straus jacket. He said, "It's an old one that I had lying around...," but he forgot to take off the tags. I didn't care if it was old or new, I quickly put it on and it gave me a new feeling...still don't know how to describe it. Farmer Browne (Francis Browne) knew of our rough times with Aquinas Academy (where Pop taught science) closing. He also knew I was providing food and paying the taxes. NOW I had a new coat. I think it was the first new coat I had ever owned and I wore it through high school and part of college years.

For my two sisters Christmas came, not only in December, but also in April, June, and September. Every couple months, Mr. Browne would bring a couple of very large boxes of girl clothes... he would say, "My daughters like the latest fashions and think these clothes are out of style." At the time, I could not figure out why the girls got so giddy when Mr. Browne pulled up to the house. Sometimes they would cry as one would pull out a new dress with tags and all. However, they'd never let on, knowing his daughters really loved shopping. Mr. Browne was so good at putting on a show, that he was not upset that his daughters would go shopping for clothes all day and then not even wear them.

The two identical shirts I wore through high school were also from Mr. Browne. One time a friend brought out four yearbooks (I couldn't believe someone purchased ALL four years of these annuals) and pointed out that I had the same shirt all four years. There I was all four years with the same shirt. I didn't know anything different and didn't care. Mom kept mending my pants with patches until everyone else in the world started to do the same. It became quite the fad back in the 60's and 70's to wear patched jeans. As I grew she would lengthen the jeans by adding a strip of cloth around the bottom of each leg. I saw that other people used guitar straps to lengthen their pants.

Mrs. Walker would call us when a dogfish came in at the herring packing plant. We found that one small shark with potatoes could feed the entire family.

That year I butchered my two beef cows for the family and went totally into dairy. It was much more work, but not only did the milk pay for the Guernseys I purchased, but paid for the grain, all the milk the family needed, and later my college tuition. The people of Fox Island appreciated the fresh milk and I always received positive comments on the thick cream it provided. The best ice cream was made from the pure cream that floated to the top of each gallon.

There was this one day that I would prefer to forget, but it too is burned into my thoughts and memories. One afternoon Mom mentioned that we were totally out of food. There wasn't anything, except a few carrots and a couple of potatoes. I had one rabbit left, but I was saving her for the litter she would provide later (we had already eaten the buck). This was the only thing I had to offer. So, I butchered her and brought it up to the kitchen. Mom quickly started into making a stew and I went back out to work on the barn. I became curious when the light started to fade and I hadn't heard the dinner bell. I kept working anyway and thought that the stew was simply taking longer than expected. Finally, after the sun had totally disappeared I walked back from the barn and entered the house. My mistake was calling out before I took in the situation. I yelled, "When's dinner?" The look on Mom's face told the story. If I had known the answer I would NEVER have said anything.

Mom had made a BIG batch of stew with my last rabbit and served it. Many of the younger boys had seconds and thirds until the stew was all GONE! I could tell my mother was feeling horrible and I felt bad for her more than being hungry. To this day I wish I could take those words back...but I can't.

I almost dropped out of school to work...but one old timer scolded me and told me to finish school. That's one of the reasons I dropped sports and went to work after school and on weekends. Joe, Tim, and John had all moved away by then and kept sending money back home. I made it my mission to make enough money to pay the taxes and most the food while finishing high school. The hayloft of the barn became my bedroom during my junior and senior years. I don't know all the details of how people helped us, but I think mom would know. I'll make it a point to ask her...

Do you remember how I said people helped each other and the mindset was, "There is always someone else having a harder time than us, so we need to help everyone?" Back then, after the great depression and war I think EVERYONE thought that way. Last year I had mentioned on the Fox Island Facebook page the above story, and here is a response I got from a dear friend, Kenny.

Kenneth D. Friermuth:

Let me tell you about the WONDERFUL Bushnell family that lived down the hill from us. When I was a senior in high school, my mother almost passed away from lung complications and was in the hospital for four months. My dad worked full time in Tacoma for a school district and would stop by after work to see her. There were five kids in my family. I was the oldest at 17; my siblings were 14, 12, 10, & 7. None of us knew how to cook, so we ate a lot of cereal, canned chili, & soup. During that time, several nights per week, a different Fox Island family had dinner prepared for us when we got home from school! Although I never tired of the tater tot hot dish we had often, I specifically remember the Bushnell's bringing our family a COMPLETE turkey dinner with all the fixings! It amazes & HUMBLES me today still when I think about the generosity these families provided us during our time of need......especially when they were providing us food they couldn't afford for their own families. They were very gracious angels in disguise!

Joe Bushnell's comments:

The Walkers sold their herring business, but were still very helpful to us when Pop lost his job when Saint Aquinas closed. I think Mrs. Walker told the new owners about our struggles in hopes that they would continue to call us when a small shark came into the plant. However, the new owners did one better, they drove their boat to our beach, hollered up to our house and all the boys came running down, then they cast their nets, caught a VERY LARGE amount of herring and gave the entire catch to us! We froze all the herring and had food for months. Dan, after you left to college they continued sending us fish for dinners...usually dogfish...but Mom had a special way of making it taste like cod.

LOST IN THE SWAMP
1973

We had some great science teachers at Peninsula High School. They would go out of their way to find hands-on projects that we could do, not only at school, but at home. Laura decided to pick some scientific experiment at Tea Swamp. A large quarter mile swamp was located deep within the woods southeast of our home. Although Laura was adventurous, she wasn't one to be playing in the woods. I had come in from milking the cows and I could tell Mom looked a bit concerned as she said, "Laura hasn't returned from Tea Swamp." All kinds of fear went through my head as I dropped the milking machine in the kitchen and RAN, not walked the mile to where I thought she might be. While heading down an overgrown logging road, I could make out a faint crying noise up ahead. It was VERY dark in the woods and I didn't take a flashlight, but really didn't need one. When I was younger I could see VERY WELL in the dark which reminds me of another story, but I digress.

As I took a left through the overgrown logging road, then down the trail I could only hear blood curdling screams. I called out to her, but my calls were drowned out by those screams. I know I should have stayed on the trail and persistently called to her, but my heart was ripped apart knowing how scared she was in those dark strange woods. Finally, she heard me and broke down into deep sobs of fear and relief. I again called to her and told her to walk in the direction of my voice, but it was too dark for her to see (I didn't know about her night blindness). So with a heavy heart, I headed off the trail and towards her voice. When I finally came to her, she slung her arms around my neck and hugged me like I had never been hugged before. Being the goofball I was/am, I said to her, "Are you lost?" She didn't seem to mind as we turned and made our way back to the old logging road.

Here is how Laura remembered the adventure:

"For the science project there were many steps that required more than one trip to the field location. Mom required me to take Dan on the first trip. I explained to Dan that I had to walk the perimeter and map the area. Dan reluctantly agreed to take me. He did an excellent job of explaining landmarks and number of steps between this tree and that stump. There was an old sectional post that was key to the direction change from into the woods to around the bog that was the outer rim of the swamp. We got to the swamp area and Dan actually stayed and helped me with converting paces to the field notes. We picked a four by four foot area and recorded all the plants on the cool graph paper that was part of the supplied with the Science Field Study kit. Dan even took me out onto the center of the bog and told me to jump. I jumped a few times and nothing happened. He encouraged me to jump again and he jumped with me. Then we stopped and could feel the bog shaking. We could also see the plant leaves quivering like in an earthquake. I made good headway of the field lab when Dan announced that we had to head back before it got dark. I whined a bit because there was still a lot of light. I was such a great seamstress, but not an outdoor adventurer. Dan must've been frustrated with my lack of common forest sense and explained that we had a lot of woods to get through to reach the road and the trees have a way of blocking out all the light. So, I packed up and we headed back. Again, Dan gave a running commentary of landmarks and the corner fence post that was the pointing me straight to the road. I was confident that I could find my way there and back again on my own.

Back in class, my science teacher announced my field notes were well organized and complete and asked, "Where are your swamp water samples?" Forehead thump. That was one important piece I had forgotten to collect. I had to get back up to Tea Swamp.

Dan told me he was sure I could get there and back on my own. I wanted to go right away when I got home from school, but it was not possible. I had kitchen chores that were not optional. I'd rather get lost in a scary, dark forest than disappoint Mom by not doing my chores. I put away all the breakfast dishes, made a salad, peeled and boiled potatoes, and set the table. I wasn't sure when the sun set, but I had all my field science gear ready to go. I left a note for Mom so she'd know where I was and took off to get my swamp water sample. I told Dan I was heading out as I passed him milking the cows. Right there was a clue that the sun was close to setting, milking the cows was a late evening chore.

Finding the swamp was just the same as my first trip. I got the water sample and stowed it carefully in my backpack. I looked up and thought unwisely that it was still really light, maybe I had time to draw the leaves of the plants in that four-by-four plot. I drew a few leaves and noticed that it was getting dark. As I headed back it was light enough at the swamp, but as soon as I got into the woods it was dark. I have one eye that doesn't see so well in the dark and this increased my difficulty. I was really scared. I counted my steps and came to the corner fence post. Heading to the road from here the ground gave way quickly downhill. I did not remember the steep descent from my trip out with Dan. I went back and tried a different direction and ran into the outer rim of the bog that surrounded the swamp, not the correct direction again. I trudged back to what I thought was the sectional post. It was totally dark by now and I had enough common sense to stay put, so I didn't get more lost or trip and twist and ankle.

I had a flashlight and a Bible. I sat down at the post and started reading from Mark. It was scary being alone in the dark, so I started reading aloud, then reading loudly to scare away any wild animals. My flashlight batteries were getting dim. To save power, I turned it off and started singing all the songs I'd learned at church guitar choir. When I heard Dan coming, I started calling out. But I was calling the same time as him, so he couldn't hear me. I had a rescue whistle, so I blew three blasts. Then Dan was quiet so he could hear me. I had the flashlight on, so he could find me. I was glad to see him. I started crying and gave him a hug that I never wanted to let go.

I had to go back for a third time. I went on a Saturday and took Dan. I really just wanted to see where I had gotten turned around. It turns out there were two fence posts, but only one that was a sectional post. I had gone to the first one that did not point the way to the road. While we walked on the old logging road, Dan found an iron pipe. It was about four feet long and two inches in diameter. "This could be useful he mused," dumping out the furch and inspecting the pipe.

"Whatever for?" I questioned.

"You never know when you can use a good solid iron pipe," Dan responded without hesitation and we continued our hike back to the county road. I got a good grade on the field science project."

THE BARN CAUGHT ON FIRE
1973

It's interesting how year after year you can do the same thing, THEN one day something happens that you remember the rest of your life. Every Wednesday I fed Mr. Browne's herd of cattle in both the BIG, tall red barn and the long short white barn. On Fridays both barn's needed cleaning and it was a huge chore...I started at 10 years old. Some of the pitch fork stabs were so heavy, I had to drag the fork with manure to the pile then dump it and get another stab. I really needed this job, for I had a goal to purchase my own beef cow someday. By the time I was in high school I was able to stab the manure and throw it out of the stall all the way to the top of the pile. Also, I had also started my own herd of dairy cows. This was just one of my many jobs. I worked week after week, month after month, and year after year. I started in 1966 and worked all the way through high school and on vacations from college at WSU.

Okay, back to the story. On this particular Wednesday, my little brother, Ed, came to help me. I told him to put the hay in the trough while I got the grain out of the white barn. As I stepped into the other barn, I just happened to glance over at him. He was standing there staring into the big red barn. I stopped and just looked at him; what could he be staring at I wondered? Just then he turned towards me with the most horrific look upon his face as he yelled, "FIRE, FIRE, FIRE!!!"

A fire in the hay barn is VERY serious! Ed ran towards me and I ran towards the tall red barn. I flung the large doors open and looked up. The ceiling had a small light bulb with the lower part wrapped in electrician's tape. The tape was burning and dripping down onto the portion of the floor with loose hay. It was spring and the bales of hay still reached the ceiling, but the barn was only half full. I climbed the stacked bales as fast as a monkey and got to the top. The problem I had is that the tape was on fire and out of my reach. I looked down to the floor 20 feet below and could see the loose hay now catching fire. No option left! I jumped off the top of the bales and flew myself out towards the light and burning tape, grabbed the whole fire source and came down. Landing on my feet in the middle of the fire I was able to stomp out. Just as I was putting out the last ember, Ed showed up with the fire extinguisher.

"Ed," I said, "that is where you went." I couldn't figure out why Ed went to the white barn, when it was the red barn that was on fire. He ran all the way through the white barn (48 feet) to the other side, grabbed the extinguisher and headed back.

While living on Fox Island I learned many lessons. Sometimes you need to call the fire department or police, sometimes you need to risk injury, and sometimes you need to risk your life to save people. Being a very agile high school farm boy, I learned that I could do many things without being injured. This was one of those times I would risk injury to save the barn and all the hay. When it came to another person's life, and after assessing the situation, I would hope I would risk my life. I have another story of when the hay field caught on fire. My sister called the fire department, but before they arrived I had the fire out and sprinklers going. I was upset at my sister, but later after thinking about it, she made the right call. I also made the right call by acting, instead of waiting.

I don't know if Ed or I ever told anyone (except Mr. Browne) about saving the barn full of hay. We did tell Mr. Browne and he said, "It's so good to have workers who will do something, rather than sit there and watch and not know what to do." Mr. Browne always found a way of making us feel very good about ourselves. He was a great role model.

You should always be prepared to do things for or by yourself. Learn to NOT rely on government to solve all your problems, and be prepared.

YOU CAN'T PLAY
1974

There were two reasons I stopped playing sports. One was in protest for a dumb rule. We won the protest and the rule was changed, but it took four years and we all suffered for not being allowed to play in our prime. The second reason was money. The school team required too much of my time, as I needed to work after school for taxes on our farm and food for our family.

While in middle school, I attended all the school dances and loved dancing the night away. I also enjoyed having my mother there as a chaperone…sure I was not a "normal" middle school boy in that regard. By the time I got to high school things really changed. The school my dad taught at closed down and he was out of a job. If I wanted to go to the dances, I'd have to pay from my own pocket, which was a blessing at the time. It wasn't like I asked for money to go to the dances, as that would be rude and selfish since we were just trying to survive from one day to the next. Once I entered high school all dancing for me, except my PE dance class, were now over.

I remember many marshmallow roasts and a pot of homemade goulash or stew over an open fire while growing up on Fox Island. Instead of going to the prom or other school dances, I would make a fire on the beach and enjoy the evening. The nights would be so soothing, with the small waves lapping, the music of the loons, and a deep and sometimes small talk of friends and family (including my mom). It wasn't until I became a vice principal and had to supervise dances did I realize I had more fun than my peers. That's what it's like growing up financially poor on Fox Island. When I was poor I had the richest experiences, but when I became "rich" I missed those experiences. I sat behind my principal's desk with flashbacks of growing up on Fox Island.

When it came to sports, well, I happen to be a very tall and strong middle schooler. At the time only one person in our entire student body was taller. I played first string football offense, defense and special teams. In basketball, I was also first string and in seventh grade we had beat every team. It was fun being a part of a winning team. My brother, John, was taller, stronger, and his arms were much longer for his body size. He was an unusually good athlete. In 1970, boys were no longer allowed to play football because their hair was too long. "Your hair can NOT touch your ears," they told us. We were also told that it's unsafe because the football helmets wouldn't stay on tight. Another coach was more honest by telling us that he didn't want any "shaggy dogs" on the team.

We thought we could make a point and make a change if we didn't play ball for the school team in protest. However, the urge to play basketball and prove the school wrong became overwhelming so we organized our own team. It was only boys who were not allowed to play for the school because their hair touched the top of their ears. WE WERE AWESOME! We signed up to play in the intramural team and didn't lose a game. Some of our team members could slam dunk the ball which I don't think was allowed, OR no one on the school team could do it. We begged the principal to allow us to play against the school team, but he wouldn't permit it.

ED ALMOST DIED
1975

In my life time things have changed a lot. In the movies, W.C. Fields would make people laugh as he drove down the highway drunk. Smokers were portrayed as being sophisticated and smart. Motorcycle riders were the "bad boys" of the earth and were always up to no good. Men would gladly lay their life down to protect women, children, and the defenseless. Most of the time men and fathers were portrayed as good and healthy, not buffoons. With that said, let me tell you a story about a drunk driver hitting my brother Ed while he was riding his motorcycle.

It happened late one night when my younger brother, Ed, was riding his motorcycle across the Tacoma Narrows Bridge. A drunk driver decided to turn his pick-up around while in the center. The cycle stopped instantly as it crumpled into the truck's side, catapulting Ed high above the deck. Although his flight lasted only seconds, his brain quickly calculated many different scenarios… "if I go over the railing, I need to grab the vertical cables to stop myself from landing in the water 600' below. If I land on the rail, I'll tuck sideways and hope to stay on this side…" Ed said, "It was eerie being in the air and having different survival ideas going through my head." He landed on his helmet and skid across the highway with feet and legs bouncing up and down off the pavement until the guardrail, on the other side cracked his helmet and helped him come to a stop. One side and part of the top of his helmet was ground down to paper thin. By the time Ed was able to stand (for his legs were shaking), he saw that the sheriff and tow truck driver had already placed his broken motorcycle in the back of the drunk's pick up and the pick-up was being towed away. Ed stood up and reported to the sheriff what had happened.

Here is how things have changed: The sheriff opened his passenger side door for the drunk driver and drove him home. Ed stood all alone, late at night, on the Tacoma Narrows Bridge, under the street lights, with no phone, no motorcycle, a broken helmet, and no ride to go the 15 – 20 miles home. As he started limping down the side of the road, a Fox Island friend recognized him, stopped, and gave him a ride home.

136

Back in the early 70's, drinking and driving was viewed much differently and motorcycle drivers were thought of as criminals (Hells Angels type). Things were much different then.

LARRY GOT RUN OVER
1975

Paul Wise and Kevin Miller looked shocked as I swore for the first (and last time). I was working with them on the old Harbor Inn when I got word that my younger brother, Larry, got run over by a drunk driver.

I wasn't the only family member who couldn't go with Mom and Pop on this HAM radio outing since I was working. The younger brothers and sisters were there. They had a great time camping with other ham radio folks and were heading back over White Pass, Mom driving the truck with Larry and Tom. Pop was way in front driving the station wagon with Tony. Everything was going just fine when all of a sudden black smoke started coming out from under the hood. Mom quickly pulled off the highway onto the large shoulder and ordered everyone out (for fear the truck would explode from the fire). As everyone bailed out, she quickly called on the truck's ham radio to Pop and explained the situation (word soon spread to ALL the hams in the area. Tom popped the hood to investigate the origin of the smoke.

Oh, I almost forgot Larry was a very good soccer player and while playing soccer a few days before someone kicked his leg and broke it. Back in those days when you break a leg they put a very large heavy plaster cast all the way from around your foot up to the top of your hip. And that is exactly what Larry was **dealing with when he got out of the smoking truck.**

As they gathered around the front of the truck someone pointed out a suspicious vehicle about half mile up the highway. It was swerving from one shoulder to the other and appeared to be heading straight for them. Mom yelled, "Get out of the way, run for it!" They headed for the deep ditch (used in the winter for snow) and up onto the high embankment. At first it seemed like everyone would make it, but the mustang was going much faster than Larry could run with his crutches. He got to the bottom of the ditch and started up the embankment before his crutches slipped out from under him and he went flat onto the ground.

Everyone was yelling to him, "COME ON LARRY, YOU CAN MAKE IT!!" Then the car took a hard left, missing the truck, shooting through the deep ditch and up the embankment where Larry was still struggling to get up. The first wheel ran over his leg, breaking the plaster cast AND his leg in a different location. The second wheel broke his arm and rib. The third wheel ran over his head breaking his nose. The car kept going a bit further, but finally hit a rock and got stuck.

My poor mother! Raising EIGHT boys has put her through life's most difficult trials. And now, to watch your child get killed right in front of you and to not be able to do anything to stop it. No one could blame her for yelling at the drunk driver as he staggered from his car (but she NEVER swore). The blood was squirting and pouring down Larry's face as he raised his head, looked at his poor defeated mother and yelled, "Shut up mom! I am not dead!" Well, if Pop had heard him talk to his mother that way he would be dead. Tom was in shock; some because they thought Larry was dead and because he talked to Mom that way.

Mom was already on her way down to him as she quickly put pressure in the right spots and started talking very calmly to Larry. Larry slowly turned his head towards the truck and saw his grandfather, who had died years before sitting there on top of the camper. He said to Larry, "It's not your time yet." Only Larry saw and heard him and didn't tell anyone for 45 years. Tom ran to the ham radio, called Pop and filled him in on the details. Pop called one of his radio friends who were all listening in disbelief while one of them called the ambulance. People didn't have cell phones back then and most people didn't have ham radios either, but we did.

Larry made it home from the hospital with a new cast on his leg, arm, and across his face to hold his nose in place. He was a wreck, but he also had seven brothers that wouldn't let him off the hook from working.

The next day we were out bailing hay and Larry wanted to work alongside of us. Well, let me allow Larry to explain what happened.

"For years I watched my older brothers working the hay fields which built in me a strong desire to do the same. After getting run over, Mom insisted I stay in the house and heal, but that's where the girls and young children were. I wanted to be out with the men working! I limped over the little bridge to Brown's farm and proceeded to grab the bales of hay with my only good hand. Dragging them to the truck, I used my good knee and hoisted it up. The dust kept getting under my mask that held my nose straight which made it harder to breathe. I was slowing the crew down and getting in the way. Farmer Brown wanted me to "go home and stay out of the way."

Brother Dan was the foreman for Mr. Brown and he was a tough taskmaster, barking out orders, insisting EVERYONE work as hard as they could, and led by example. No one could out work Dan, except maybe Mr. Brown, and Dan would let everyone know it. Although he was tough on the outside, we all knew he was a real softy, especially if he knew you were doing your best. Dan saw that I was crushed when Mr. Brown told me to go home. He quickly said, "Larry, you're driving the truck!" It was hard letting out the clutch while my leg was in a full cast, not to mention steering.

Farmer Brown said something like, "He doesn't have a license" which was odd since he allowed Dan to drive from one farm to the next years before he got a license.

Dan just barked back, "I'll drive the truck to the barn and around the buildings." I really appreciate brother Dan defending me. He always put on the act that he was the tough boss, but he was a real soft hearted brother."

After the long day of haying, we celebrated with a baseball game. The crew from Tacoma called us the Fox Island Dingle Weeders. However, we named them the Tacoma City Slickers. At first they insisted Larry play baseball, even though he was injured, but after a few homeruns they started having second thoughts. Larry was a good athlete as most of us boys were. Although he could only bat with one good arm, it was still better than anything the Slickers could bring to the plate. That day the Fox Island Dingle Weeders beat the Tacoma City Slickers 18 to 0. I think the score was higher, but we just stopped counting and kept running.

THE HAYFIELD CAUGHT ON FIRE
1975

"Common farm sense was not strong in this one," I remember my mother telling me after a week with Aweso, our Japanese exchange student. Larry discovered a love for the Japanese language so he signed up to be an exchange student for 12 months and we…well, we got Aweso.

It was summer time and the hay in one of Mr. Browne's orchards needed mowing. The morning of the fire I had already milked the cows, cleaned the barns, and picked up around my barn while burning the garbage. I had started the small fire with the garbage and was throwing more small wood scraps on. Remembering I still had to cut the hay and the dew had already disappeared, I told Aweso to watch the fire while I went and cut the hay in the orchard. "OOKAAYA!" So I backed the old 1940's cub out of the barn and headed for the orchard. The field was just over the hill from the location of the small fire, so I couldn't see it from there, but I had no worries, Aweso was watching it.

I had cut the perimeter of the orchard and started down the rows. I had to concentrate when mowing the orchard, since I had to go around all the trees. Back and forth I went, row after row, BUT something was different every time I came back to the north side. More smoke seemed to come from my small fire every time I looked. "Well," I thought, "Aweso must be picking up scraps and burning them for me." I wasn't too keen on that since I only wanted a small fire that day due to the dry hay field just south of the barn. "I'll take one more pass through the orchard and if there's more smoke I'll take a look." Sure enough it became obvious my "small fire" was no longer small. I saw a lot of smoke.

I jumped off the tractor, and left it sitting in the orchard as I took off running to the crest of the hill. Looking down, I was in disbelief to see a fire nearly two hundred feet long and 50 feet wide. Aweso was still sitting there watching the fire. I can't remember touching the ground as I ran, my heart pumping adrenalin to every muscle I had. The fire was too big for

141

one man, so I ran right through it all the way to the house. As I opened the front sliding glass door I bellowed, "FIRE, FIRE, GET THE HOSES!!!!" Then I ran back down. Ed, Tom, Mary and Laura were home and poured out of the house to help. I got back down and started putting it out.

We were all COVERED with black soot as I pulled hoses and sprinklers over to the still smoldering black patch. I was in shock as I looked over to Aweso as he was STILL sitting there watching. I yelled, "Aweso, why didn't you watch the fire! I asked you to keep an eye on it?"

"I did watch, it got bigger and bigger...BIG FIRE!" Then I remembered my mother's warning, "Aweso is not one with a lot of farm common sense." Just then the fire trucks pulled up,

"OH, who would call and bother them I said loudly."

Mary said, "I did."

"Mary, why? Now they might charge us money we don't have!" I knew that minute I was out of line and felt bad as she was only doing what made sense. Who knows, if the wind had picked up it would have spread to Mr. Browne's fields. Oh, that was a close one!!! I told Mary to go tell them that the fire is all taken care of and they can leave. I took a walk and followed the charred perimeter and saw that it had gone right up to my 1962 VW bug, stopped, went around the bug and towards the old barn. We were able to stop the fire within two feet of the barn. The Lord took care of my car, my barn and the field.

So, after turning on the sprinklers, asking Ed to keep an eye on the burned area, I went back to cutting the orchard. By the way, after one area was soaked, Ed moved the sprinkler to soak another area. This was something I didn't have to tell a farm boy.

Fox Island was a great incubator of lessons. We did not rely on the government to solve our problems. When something was on fire, you put it out. When someone is hurt or is in need, you helped. It's just the way things were back then, growing up on Fox Island.

CLOTH NAPKINS
1975

I remember going to the A & W restaurant one time. I was in third grade and Mrs. Ford was driving a bunch of us children home from basketball practice when she decided to take us to Tacoma to buy root beer floats. It was so awesome!!!! She bought me a large root beer float...never had one before!!! Coming from a family of 12 we couldn't afford going out to eat. The next time I went to a restaurant it was a surprise high school graduation dinner with some of my teachers: George and Roberta Palo, Paul and Pamela Wise, Kevin Miller and his wife. Needless to say, I watched their every move so I could figure out how to eat at a fancy joint. I had some fabulous teachers at Peninsula High School who really cared about me and all their students. That was the first and last time I went to a fancy restaurant until I started working at one to earn money for my third year of college.

This photo reminds me of how I felt trying to figure out how to eat properly at a restaurant.

I had decided to skip out on my graduation ceremony since you needed to purchase a cap and gown. Why spend the money when your family really needed it? My good friend and teacher, Pam Wise found out and talked to a friend and fellow classmate of mine, Heidi. Evidently her brother graduated the year before me and still had his cap and gown and he would be glad to give it to me. I declined, but somehow my mother found out and told me, "Graduation isn't about YOU! It has more to do with all the people who love you and got you to this place. So, before you let them all down, you just think about the decision you are making." I NEVER thought of it that way and definitely never wanted to let my friends down, so there I was at graduation.

While sitting there at graduation, minding my own business I saw my good friend, Pam Wise, walk up to the podium. She scanned the crowd of green clad graduates until her eyes met mine. The parents and graduates all hushed as she started into her speech, much like a master conductor starting an orchestra. Her voice demonstrated confidence and commanded everyone's attention. THEN right in the middle of her speech, she mentioned my name and some of the accomplishments I had made. I was dumbfounded! To this day I remember the public adulation she bestowed on this one young boy. It was those few words of public encouragement that I remembered during finals week at college when I just wanted to give up. It was her words that kept me going when all the other college students were out playing or partying while I was trying to finish reading the books.

One day I mentioned to my good friend and mentor, Paul Wise, that I was thinking about going to college. However, I told him I couldn't read. The hammer he was using just froze in mid-air. "How can that be?" he said in a shocked voice. "You're in tenth grade and you have great grades."

I replied, "I know, but I can listen very well and figure things out when I need to. However, I am not good at reading."

Paul left me alone for a while as I continued working on his house. Evidently he went and made some phone calls because when I went back to school George cornered me, pointed at a poster on the wall and asked me to read it. I did read it to him. "See, you can read!" he pointed out.

I said, "Well, yes I can read, but it really takes me a long time and I can't really read out loud at all."

Roberta Palo offered to help me if I'd stop by her elementary class after school. I didn't take her up on that offer, but instead I signed up for a remedial reading class at the high school. At that point in my life I didn't care what my peers thought, I just wanted to be a better reader! The teacher tested me and I came out at the fourth grade second month level. I wanted to be a better reader so badly that I took a book (The Hobbit and others like it) and read EVERYDAY for one hour, seven days a week, ALL

YEAR. I really didn't understand what I was reading, but I read the words. In the remedial reading class, the teacher started me at my reading grade level (and got out of the way). She had thousands of books on a microfilm/filmstrip projector that I could read at my level, then turn a knob to make the sentences pass by faster as I improved. I took reading VERY SERIOURLY! In one semester I had completed a year's worth of reading, but I kept reading anyway. After one year I had completed two years of reading. At home I continued my reading regiment by sitting for an hour a day attempting to understand the Lord of the Rings trilogy. This continued for three years and by the end of my senior year I was reading at grade level.

Now you may understand why Pamela Wise made such a big impression on me when giving her speech. It was those words and words from my other teachers that kept encouraging me as I struggled to keep up in college.

My first semester of college, I got a 1.9 GPA and was put on probation. However, I worked harder and continued to struggle through reading all those textbooks, got off probation and by my senior year I was pulling a 3.5 GPA. I kept working hard and NEVER gave up. I credit my success squarely onto the shoulders of my good teachers. Whenever I felt discouraged I would think of those teachers who had faith in me.

My teachers made such a good impression, that I too became a teacher, then a principal! I was able to pass it forward MANY times...I just loved them. Back in 1979, I had Mr. Palo, Mr. Miller, and Mr. Wise as groomsmen at my wedding. My bride thought I was weird, but now, after 40 years...well maybe I am, BUT, I had fabulous teachers!

Grandchildren, listen to me: Friends are like mycelium in a person's life, they can build you up or pull you down, so choose them wisely.

LISTEN TO YOUR PARENTS
1975

Pop advised my brother to keep his $2,000 trust fund for college. He explained that it could cover all his educational needs, a dream most people would love to live. But my brother had a different idea. When he turned 18 he took the money and bought a like new cherry red jeep. I don't remember my dad EVER buying a new near car and NEVER spent over $1,000 for one. Fact is, the land Pop bought from the kelp line back quarter mile only cost $1,500 and the two story five bedroom house that he had built cost $15,000. To pay $2,000 for a car was foolish, but he didn't listen to Pop.

My brother was so excited to drive it, he paid the money, got behind the wheel and drove home. He was really looking mighty fine in that almost new red jeep. Well, he was looking good until the sheriff pulled up to our house and asked for him. He was a bit bewildered as the sheriff explained that the car was reported stolen. My brother was shocked, "But I JUST bought it today from Slime." (Not his real name.)

The sheriff replied, "Oh, if you purchased it from him that's simple, show me the bill of sale."

He replied, "What's a bill of sale?"

The sheriff, who happened to be a friend, started to get worried as he said, "Okay, just give me the title transfer."

Now my brother started to look worried, "Title what? Transfer? What's that?"

The sheriff rolled his eyes and said, "You didn't talk with your dad before you purchased this car did you!" He shook his head and said, "Well, my dad told me to save my money for college, but I just wanted that Jeep.

Just then the person my brother purchased the car from pulled up. "Oh you found my car, thank you." The sheriff asked Slime a lot of questions, including what should be done now. The guy just said, "Nothing, I am just glad I got my car back." My brother was more relieved than upset, since back then if you steal a car you would be put in jail for a VERY LONG TIME. It was called Grand Theft Auto!

Well, Slime left and the sheriff could only say, "Perhaps next time you should listen to your parents."

A couple years before robbing my brother, Slime had sued the government for mega bucks and now it was almost all gone. So he stole from my brother, but that's not the end of this low life's story. Slime discovered a young lady with special needs that was living by herself. She had a lot of money and you guessed it, he schmoozed his charm on her. No one ever showed her interest before and this was like a dream come true. Her parents warned her to keep away from him. It turned more into a nightmare for her when he got into her bank account, stole ALL the money, and disappeared. Slime took off to Arizona, but no one really knew where he went. That is, no one except one guy.

As you may know, we have brother who was a logger and knew some very rough men as he was growing up. One of his friends, which I will call Duke, was a muscle bound, tough, old time logger. Duke made my tough brother look like a pansy. When my brother told Duke what Slime had done to our other brother he became very upset. Duke happened to be the one guy who knew where the jerk lived and decided to deal with him. Although none of my brothers had any idea what Duke was thinking.

Duke drove to Arizona and moved in with Slime ball, all the while scheming of ways to get even. While in Arizona, Duke and Slime lived a wild, tough life, but eventually the opportunity presented itself. One day Slime asked Duke if he would harm someone in Arizona. Duke said he wouldn't do it until Slime paid him a million dollars in cash. Within an hour of receiving the money, Duke took off and Slime never saw him again. And that's how Duke got even with Slime, although my brother never got his $2,000 back.

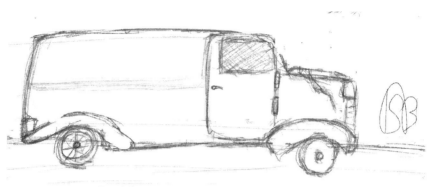

RETIRING THE BLUE BOMB
1976

Just as there are many more stories to be written about the history of growing up on Fox Island there are many more stories about the Dodge Panel. Several of my brothers have cut their automotive mechanical teeth on the Blue Bomb. It always seemed to end up in the bushes, just sitting there waiting for the next brother to take it over.

One time the State Patrol officer pulled us over because the Bomb only had one tail light. Well, Mom explained, "When Pop and I purchased this 1948 panel truck it only came with one tail light." So the officer looked inside; I think trying to determine its age. He asked Mom to try the horn and she again explained that in 1948 it was not required to have a horn. Next, he asked if he could check the brakes and thankfully Mom had asked Ed if he would fix them for her just a week before. So, the officer left and Mom didn't get a ticket.

In the early 70's the license plate was getting very hard to read, so Mom took some enamel paint and went over the lettering and numbers so they would show up better. The State Patrol stopped her again, but she didn't get a ticket. After agreeing that the paint job was an improvement, she went and purchased a new license plate anyway.

Looking back only makes me laugh more, since WHO ELSE drove that truck around Fox Island/ Gig Harbor anyway? Who really needed a license plate? LOL

Laura's memory:

One time Dan, Tom and I got up very early on a Saturday morning to go fishing off the old cement dock. It came to an abrupt end when Tom accidently pulled the fishing line that Dan was holding and put the fish hook through the web of Dan's hand. He didn't do it on purpose and Tom was scared that Dan would be mad. However, to our utter astonishment, he was not. He just looked wide eyed and made small little wheezing sounds, like he was gasping for air. Well, we rode all the way to Madigan Hospital in the Blue Bomb.

Mom used it to get to work at Harbor Heights Elementary School. We had to take blankets to wrap around us. I thought it was like riding in a horse drawn wagon, but with exhaust smell instead of horse. She is such a great trooper...it was like she was saying to the world, "You can have your fancy cars, I'll take having children over being rich any day! And my quiver is full." We all are so proud of her!

I remember in 1974 Mom had to drive Ed to several small independent auto parts shops to look for parts for the Blue Bomb. The parts needed were so old they were not listed in inventory and we had to physically look through parts bins.

Another time, while Joe was still in high school and before he graduated in 1969, he use to park in front of PHS (it was called, "The Blue Bomber" back then). Some troublemakers rolled the Bomb over the hillside in front of the school. It went all the way down the hill and turned over. With the help of Joe's friends and many of the good kids, they righted the indestructible truck and he drove away! The Blue Bomb was so well built and the metal was so thick that the "rollover" didn't cause any damage.

Ed was 15 when he took over the THIRD revival of the Blue Bomb. He was/is a FABULOUS mechanic!! When I say worked on it, I am talking about tearing the engine all the way down to the block and rebuilding it.

Next he decided to try and get the old panel timed just right, so without the proper timing tools he used an old farmer's trick. Ed sat on the left front fender with the hood folded up, Mike Ford hooked a chain from Pop's pickup truck to the front of the Blue Bomb, and Larry steered the Bomb. Mike got up to 35 mph (usually on the downhill side of 14th) while Ed patiently poured gas into the carburetor and turned the distributor until the old 1948 Dodge panel started coughing, kicking, and finally sputtered to life. Please note: while Ed was pouring gas into the carb and turning the distributor, he was sitting on the front right fender while traveling 35 mph.... Again, look at the photo and you'll see how crazy that was. Jim Kimble gave Ed a crank from his farm which fit in the front harmonic balancer and he used it to crank start the old truck. Ed drove that truck everywhere until he decided he wanted more speed.

Many years later, Tony recalled his babysitter asking Mom if the "Blue Bomb" was still running. Mom replied, "No, but it had a sad end to a well lived life." The panel truck was pulled out to the field and parked. When the taxes got too high, and Mom and Pop retired they too were forced to move from their paradise island, to be tucked away in a distant town where the cost of living was much lower. As they left their home for the last time and passed every corner, every tree, every fencepost, a glance over at the Blue Bomb had sent a nostalgic thought. Would their history on Fox Island also be lost in the brambles of time along with their first family car.

ABOUT THE AUTHOR

Daniel Bushnell grew up on Fox Island and has been in education for over 40 years as a teacher, administrator, & professor. He lives in Lake Stevens, Washington, with his wonderful wife. They raised four daughters and currently have 13 grandchildren.

Made in the USA
Columbia, SC
13 April 2019